Say What!?

Crazy Things Jesus Might Say, If We Would Listen

Jack Hilligoss

sermonto**book**
.com

Sermon To Book
www.sermontobook.com

Say What!? / Jack Hilligoss
ISBN-13: 9780692690918
ISBN-10: 0692690913

Dedicated to Bill and Barbara Hilligoss. You were great parents and better Christians. You helped me love God, His Word, and His church. And also, to my dear friends John and Jinny Laderer: Thank you for encouraging me to listen to Jesus and follow the dream.

CONTENTS

What Jesus Looked Like

"What did Jesus look like?"

That question appeared in my Facebook feed early last Christmas season, and I followed the attached link. I hate to admit to you how much time I spend on Facebook, but this article was about Jesus, so I felt it was my duty as clergy to read it. The opening lines were a series of additional questions:

"Was he blond like Brad Pitt? Was he black like Kanye 'Yeezus' West? Just what did Jesus Christ look like?"

I will save you some time. The article concluded that no one knows what Jesus looked like. However, it shared an interesting story about a recent depiction of Jesus created by a British scientist and Israeli archeologists that they say is the most accurate image of Jesus ever made. While they were clear that no one can say exactly what Jesus looked like, they were just as clear in saying that he certainly did not look like the image we routinely see in pictures hanging on the walls of Christian bookstores, churches, and homes. You probably knew that.

Still, we all have some image of Jesus in our minds. It floats there in our imagination while we are singing praises or whispering prayers to Him. I think that is normal. I also think it can be very dangerous.

My wife has a "thing" for Mel Gibson. I can't understand it myself, but what are you going to do? Some women go for guys with square jaws, smoldering eyes, well-defined ab muscles, and lots of money. Go figure. Still, while I am aware that she finds Mel attractive, I am confident of her love for me. She often makes it a point to tell me she loves me, and I find that reassuring. However, if I were to walk into our bedroom to discover that she had removed our "We are blessed" wall plaque and replaced it with a poster of Mel in his *Braveheart* kilt, that would be a problem.

Take the scenario further and imagine with me that at the beginning of every day or the end of each evening, she would kiss that picture of Mel and say: "I love you so much, Jack. You are the best, Jack. I wouldn't take anyone over you, Jack." Do you think I would feel that she loved me? She could protest that she was loving me, but she would actually be hurting and dishonoring me by using my name to love the image of another man. I would be experiencing what the Bible calls idol worship.

When we say we are worshipping God or loving Jesus but we have substituted our image or thoughts for who

He really is, we are committing idolatry. I think many of us are doing that without realizing it. We open our Bibles, say our prayers, and do our devotionals, all while uttering the name of Jesus but loving an image that is not Jesus. There are several of these images that we create.

One image of Jesus that has been engraved into our thinking is of a legalistic life coach who left us a list of duties that we must accomplish daily in a prescribed fashion to stay in His good graces and unlock blessings. Another image is of a concerned and easygoing friend who is on call to help us fulfill important life goals that we have set for ourselves. The list could go on and on. The false images are too numerous to be addressed in any one work. However, this reality doesn't have to become a reason for giving up trying to better know Jesus.

D. Stuart Briscoe is a prolific Christian author and teacher who has pastored an evangelical church in Wisconsin for years. He began his first career as a banker. During his training, he asked if he would be taught how to spot the marks of counterfeit money. The trainer responded that the best way to learn to spot counterfeit money was to become so familiar with the look and feel of real money that anything counterfeit would immediately stand out. Briscoe stated that this should be the approach to knowing Jesus as believers. We cannot take all the time necessary to familiarize ourselves with every counterfeit image of Christ, but we can become so familiar with the real Jesus that we are immediately sensitive to any counterfeits that come to us with His name attached.

That is my motivation for writing this book. I want us to become much more familiar with the genuine Jesus and His words. More specifically, I want to deal with the things Jesus said about areas of life that I most often have to help people process as the pastor of a local church. Believers approach me with tons of questions (don't let this out, but it stuns me that they have that level of confidence in me). The questions come to me in a myriad of ways, but after nearly thirty years, I think that I can gather them up into three main categories:

- How do I deepen my relationship with God?
- How do I discern God's will for a particular life choice or decision? (I will speak directly to the choice of a spouse in this book.)
- What does it really mean to "follow Jesus" in my circumstances and life?

These three questions cover the primary areas of concern, and I have concluded that a great deal of the frustration and confusion we experience in wrestling with them is the result of images and ideas of Jesus and His will that have nothing to do with what Jesus really said.

In order to introduce you to the idea of breaking down your accidental idol and dealing with the real Jesus, this book will tackle specific topics that come up in those three areas, and we will walk together through the actual words of Jesus that address those questions. Section 1 focuses on deepening our relationship with Him through prayer, Scripture reading, and the like. Section 2 deals with areas of discerning God's will. The final section examines what we mean and what Jesus means when He tells us to follow Him.

Each chapter title is a summation of the specific teaching we will concentrate on in that chapter. I purposefully chose these titles to act as hammers on the cultural ideas that may need to be shattered in our thinking.

I hope this little book gives you the tools you need to expand your idol smashing, now and in the future.

CHAPTER ONE

When Jesus Talks

Jesus and his disciples went on to the villages around Caesarea Philippi. On the way he asked them, "Who do people say I am?" They replied, "Some say John the Baptist; others say Elijah; and still others, one of the prophets."

"But what about you?" he asked. "Who do you say I am?"

Peter answered, "You are the Messiah."

Jesus warned them not to tell anyone about him.

He then began to teach them that the Son of Man must suffer many things and be rejected by the elders, the chief priests and the teachers of the law, and that he must be killed and after three days rise again. He spoke plainly about this, and Peter took him aside and began to rebuke him.

But when Jesus turned and looked at his disciples, he rebuked Peter. "Get behind me, Satan!" he said. "You do not have in mind the concerns of God, but merely human concerns."

Then he called the crowd to him along with his disciples and said: "Whoever wants to be my disciple must deny themselves and take up their cross and follow me. For

> *whoever wants to save their life will lose it, but whoever loses their life for me and for the gospel will save it. What good is it for someone to gain the whole world, yet forfeit their soul? Or what can anyone give in exchange for their soul? If anyone is ashamed of me and my words in this adulterous and sinful generation, the Son of Man will be ashamed of them when he comes in his Father's glory with the holy angels."* — **Mark 8:27-38 (NIV)**

"Jesus is Selling Out…" That Internet article headline caught my attention. Being a preacher, this possibility concerned me. I am used to politicians selling out, but I have learned to trust Jesus. Still, I read the article and found that it was true. Jesus was indeed selling out…at Walmart, Target, and other retail stores.

It turns out that a toy company had created a line of twelve-inch-tall action figures called "Messengers of Faith." These dolls are made in the image of biblical characters like Moses, Sampson, and David. One of the action figures was a Jesus doll, which had a unique feature: It could talk. If a child pushed a button, the Jesus doll would recite "sixty-three seconds of scripture, recorded in an easy to memorize style." Jesus's talking is where the trouble began.

One customer who bought the Jesus doll on Amazon wrote in her review that "the voice of Jesus is a little loud." When the company that manufactured the Talking Jesus Doll tried to donate four hundred of them to the Marine Corps for their "Toys for Tots" Christmas drive, they were turned down. The "Toys for Tots" spokesperson explained: "We have to be everything for everybody. The kids we are helping could be celebrating

Christmas, Hanukkah, or Kwanzaa. There's always a chance that giving them a doll that cites scripture would be inappropriate."

So it wasn't the Jesus doll they had a problem with; it was what the Jesus doll said that caused the issue. It seems as though that has always been the case. Not just with the doll, but with the real Jesus. That is probably why he said, "If anyone is ashamed of me and my words" (Mark 8:38 NIV). Most people don't have a problem with Jesus until He starts talking.

Jesus had asked, "Who do people say I am?" (Mark 8:27 NIV), and He wasn't doing too badly in the public opinion polls. His disciples told Him, "Some say John the Baptist; others say Elijah; and still others, one of the prophets" (Mark 8:28 NIV). That is some heady company for a Jewish rabbi. Jesus was breathing some rarified air.

Not much has changed over the centuries. By and large, people still hold pretty high opinions of Jesus. They may not care for religion or the church, but you won't find many people who just don't like Jesus. They will say he was a great man, a great teacher, and a wonderful religious leader. They will acknowledge the influence he has had on the good in our world. Even people deeply committed to religions other than Christianity speak highly of Jesus. So far, so good.

Then Jesus gets personal: "But what about you?…Who do you say I am?" (Mark 8:29 NIV).

Peter made a bold declaration of faith in Jesus. Most of you have probably done that as well. You probably agree with Peter that Jesus is God's Messiah and our

Savior. If you are a Christian, you also acknowledge that He is God incarnate and the only way of salvation. We profess this, and we can be militant about our beliefs when it comes to Jesus.

I pastor a church in the Bible Belt. If you ask the average professing Christian in our neck of the woods if they're ashamed of Jesus, then you better duck! They will respond very passionately, "Of course not. He is my Lord and Savior." Around here we wear camouflage T-shirts that say "Real men love Jesus," and we have more fish magnetically attached to our cars than are swimming in the Atlantic Ocean. We listen to Contemporary Christian Radio, and we sat in line for hours to buy a sandwich at Chick-fil-A when Mr. Cathy stood up against the gay lobby. We are definitely not ashamed of Jesus Christ, so Jesus is doing all right. People tend to think of Him pretty favorably, but then He has to go and talk!

Mark says, "He spoke plainly..." (Mark 8:32 NIV). And immediately, Peter, who had just made such an admirable confession, pulled Jesus aside and began to dress Him down: "Jesus, our 'Christ,' our 'messiah,' is supposed to liberate Israel and make us rulers in the new Kingdom. So this talk about rejection, suffering, crucifixion, you need to knock that off."

But Jesus didn't stop talking—wouldn't stop telling the truth—and suddenly He wasn't all that popular anymore. If a god wants to stay popular, it is best for him not to talk.

...their idols are silver and gold, made by human hands. They have mouths, but cannot speak, eyes, but cannot see.
— **Psalm 115:4-5 (NIV)**

Like a scarecrow in a cucumber field, their idols cannot speak... — **Jeremiah 10:5 (NIV)**

We want gods who protect our stuff but stay out of our business. Nobody wants a God who actually watches what we do and speaks to correct how we live. However, that option is not available to people who call themselves Christians. If you say that your relationship to Christ is based upon what He did for you but you do not live according to the words that He spoke to you, then the cross you wear around your neck is just a graven image. You are worshipping an idol. We must not be ashamed of Him or His words (Mark 8:38).

The Words Are the Problem

It is strange how we humans can love people and still be ashamed of them. My wife's father was the pastor of the First Church of God in a small town where she attended high school. Most mornings, she would ride the bus, but there were occasions when her dad would drive her. This was mortifying because he commuted about town in the church's fifteen-passenger van that had the name of the congregation painted on its side panels in huge block letters. In her mind, it attracted attention like a cat would at a dog show. She would beg her father to drop her off a block away rather than drive her right up to the curb.

I know my wife loved her dad—no doubt about that—but there was something in her heart and the atmosphere that also embarrassed her. It can happen to us. We can love Jesus and profess Him as our Savior but still be a little uneasy about how people will respond to His words.

Jesus called our generation "adulterous" and "sinful." Where does Jesus get off calling anything sinful? Isn't the whole idea of "sin" just a little outdated? We live in a world where nothing is really a sin. To call anything sin just betrays ignorance and intolerance. There is no sin; there are just alternative truths, alternative values, and alternative lifestyles. But Jesus had the audacity to call some things sinful. He talked about adultery, unforgiveness, stealing, and exploiting others for personal advantage and gain. Jesus didn't just speak about evil in general: He had the gall to get specific. He said that there is right and wrong, true and false, acceptable and unacceptable lifestyles, and some behaviors are good and some are evil. In many places, He said it in very specific ways.

What is even more outrageous is that He said our response to his words would be the basis of our judgment in eternity. If we are ashamed of Him and His words, then God will be ashamed of us when He returns. Do you believe this guy? Jesus is imposing His truth on us. It's one thing to say you personally believe some things are good and others evil. However, Jesus imposes His words on us. He actually has the nerve to tell us that our destiny rides on how we respond to His words. That is absolutely against the rules! Not only is it socially repugnant, but also you will never keep a TV show on HGTV if you do that.

For those of us who cut their teeth in Sunday school, it is difficult to comprehend how incredible some of the things that Jesus said had sounded to the original disciples—how crazy they still sound to non-Christians today. Really listen to what Jesus says. Shut off your "Sunday-go-to-meeting" mind, turn on your "real" mind, and ask yourself: Doesn't all this apocalyptic talk about God's glory and holy angels sound a little crazy?

But you don't even have to dwell on the strange words. Just look at what He said plainly. He taught them that He would suffer, be rejected and murdered, and then be resurrected from the dead in three days (Mark 8:31). Mark says He spoke about these things "plainly." In other words, they understood what He was saying; they just couldn't believe it or accept it. It has never been easy. Decades later, Paul wrote, "We preach Christ crucified: a stumbling block to the Jews and foolishness to the Gentiles" (1 Corinthians 1:23 NIV). Jesus said things, made claims, and we ask people to believe things that are difficult and seem foolish.

They offend the human intellect and cross the boundaries of common sense. We shouldn't deny it. Jesus knew it, and He knew this would tempt us to be a little sheepish, a little self-conscious, and a little ashamed of His words. But that is not the biggest problem.

Jesus's Words Are a Personal Problem

Jesus's words are a problem; however our reaction to them can be a bigger problem. It is an enjoyable sport for us to share about this "adulterous and sinful" world. If Jesus had focused solely on those people, everybody would have shouted, "Amen! Sick 'em, Rabbi," and gone home for fried chicken and a nap. But what prompted Jesus to issue the warning in this passage weren't the actions of an unbeliever, but the resistance of a believer.

Peter took Jesus aside and tried to silence Him. Jesus responded, "Get behind me, Satan! You do not have in mind the concerns of God, but merely human concerns."

You know it is tough when Jesus has to point out the devil in you. You can love Jesus and think you are doing everything right, but the devil could be using you to try to derail God's plans. It is hard for us to detect this activity in our lives, but Jesus gives us a clue. He points out that we are in trouble when we try to resist God's truth under the pretense that we are serving Him.

Jesus plainly spoke that He would be rejected and crucified. He was not asking for opinions or alternatives; He was telling them and us what *must* happen. He made it perfectly clear and detailed. Peter simply didn't like what Jesus said, so he appealed to Him. I am certain he tried to make Jesus understand that he had His best in mind, but Jesus called it the devil in Peter.

Along with Peter, those of us who claim that Jesus is Savior have this amazing ability to resist and rationalize the things He says must be done. Jesus said we must forgive up to seventy times seven times and we must do good to people who mistreat us. He taught believers to give a substantial portion of our material goods to the poor and that we must value Him above our political and commercial affiliations. Jesus told us that we must honor our marriage vows, be intentionally engaged in trying to make disciples, and be sexually pure in both action and thought. These are nonnegotiable, but we hear them and want to negotiate. Like Peter, in one breath we say, "You are the Christ; You are my God," but then in the next we say, "Wait a minute, Jesus, I am not sure I am ready to accept Your words."

Jesus's words give us pause, especially such words as: "If anyone would come after me, he must deny himself and take up his cross and follow me" (Mark 8:34 NIV). There is that word *must* again. Jesus had just said, "I am so committed to the will of the Father that I will do whatever He tells me to do to fulfill His purpose, even the cross." When He said we must take up our cross, He was saying we need to have the same attitude. We must be so committed to the words of Jesus that we will do whatever He says, even if it means the death of our personal desires. Remember that our biggest enemy isn't the opposition we see in the world around us: It is the devil we can't see in ourselves. Jesus's words are the nails that fasten our selfishness on the cross.

When His words address a relationship we are involved in, the selfishness in us wants and needs that companionship. When His words address the way we treat our employees, our pride wants to rebel. When His words shine light on our bitterness, we want to justify and refuse to forgive. When His words address our materialism, we don't want to give up some of our stuff in order to be obedient and generous. When His words do these things, we all want to pull Jesus aside and try to get Him to change His mind. But He still asks, "Why do you call Me Lord, and do not do the things that I say?"

Jesus's Words Are Critical

One of the traits that I find so admirable in Christ is that He bothered to explain things to us. He knew we would put up resistance or not understand His ways. He took the time to give us the reason and the rationale behind the words that He spoke. He did that in this interaction, and the reasons He gave for His absolute demand that we keep His words are critical to our faith and our lives.

Jesus's Words Determine Our Quality of Life

A few summers ago, our family rented a beautiful home on the banks of a mountain lake in North Carolina. Each morning would begin with my wife and I sitting on the back deck watching the sunrise over the lake as we drank a fresh-brewed cup of coffee. We would breathe the air and listen to birds welcome the day as we made plans for the unhurried activities we would enjoy with our kids that day. Every morning at some point in that conversation, one of us would blissfully exhale: "this is what I call living."

You've used that line before or heard it used. You understand that it doesn't mean "my heart is beating, my blood is circulating, all my biological functions seem good, so I must be living." It is not a comment on the fact of life but on the quality of the moment, the sheer satisfaction and joy that fill the time. That is what Jesus was referring to when He said, "For whoever wants to save his life will lose it, but whoever loses his life for me and for the gospel will save it" (Mark 8:35 NIV). He was addressing our experience of life as much as our actual living. Our commitment to His words impacts our appreciation and enjoyment of life.

Most of the choices we make or refuse to make are influenced by us trying to save our lives—trying to protect ourselves, maintain our standard of living, be happy, feel secure, and have at least a little fun. Listen to the laundry lists of typical excuses you hear when people are called to follow and serve:

- "I need to save my weekends for personal projects."
- "I have to save enough for retirement, so I cannot be as generous as I would like."
- "I have a reputation to think about (read *save*), so I will remain silent on this controversy."

We try desperately to protect and secure all the things we think will make us happy. Jesus comes along and tells us to do the exact opposite: "Don't try to save your life. Quit being so guarded, suspicious, nervous, and worried. Give freely, sacrifice for others, and don't try to defend your life. Do what I say and you will find real life."

Jesus words certainly, and in unexpected ways, impact the quality of life we experience.

Jesus's Words Shape Our Souls

One of the reasons we underestimate the power and influence of words is because we still don't live as if we understand that we have a soul. There is an eternal and immaterial part of each of us that cannot be sustained by oxygen, food, money, sex, or power. Your soul is fed and shaped by the beliefs you adopt and live by. Scripture makes it clear that God is working in all of our circumstances to conform us to the image of Christ. But there are also forces working on our souls in the opposite direction.

> Good and evil both increase at compound interest. That is why the little decisions you and I make every day are of such infinite importance. The smallest good act today is the capture of a strategic point from which, a few months later, you may be able to go on to victories you never dreamed of. An apparently trivial indulgence in lust or anger today is the loss of a ridge or railway line or bridgehead from which the enemy may launch an attack otherwise impossible. — **C. S. Lewis**[1]

This truth is why Jesus said that if we pursue life on our own, we will make decisions that cause us to forfeit our souls. On the other hand, obedience to His words expands and shapes our souls for another world.

I was invited to speak at the Convention of the Church of God in the island nation of Cayman. Cayman is located in a breathtaking crystal-clear spot of the Caribbean Sea. On one of the days of the convention, my host gave me the opportunity to go snorkeling at a place called Eden's Rock. You can see straight down to the sea floor off of Eden's Rock. As you snorkel there, clouds of multicolored fish will swim around and past you on all sides. You can spy sea turtles and dolphins. It is a sensory smorgasbord.

However, if that's what I was going to experience, then I had to listen closely. I had never been snorkeling in my life, so as we made our way there, my friend gave me detailed instructions on how to put on the mask, use the tube, and dive with a mask on, plus several other critical concepts. In order to experience and enjoy this gorgeous underwater world, I had to listen and apply his instructions in my normal world.

Jesus's words are the instructions that prepare us in this world to be the kind of people who will be able to thrive in and enjoy eternity.

Jesus's Words Determine Our Destiny

If we are ashamed of Him and His words in this world, He will be ashamed of us when He comes again (Mark 8:38). Those are the words of Jesus.

For the remainder of this book, we are going to look at the things Jesus said that will certainly challenge our way of thinking and the commitment we may have taken for granted. I hope you will read intently, but moreover, that you will listen to see if the living Christ has something to say directly to your heart.

Chapter 1 Notes

_____

_____

_____

_____

_____

_____

_____

_____

_____

_____

_____

_____

_____

_____

_____

_____

_____

_____

_____

_____

_____

_____

_____

CHAPTER TWO

Reading the Bible Isn't Good Enough

*You diligently study the Scriptures because you think that by them you possess eternal life. These are the Scriptures that testify about me, yet you refuse to come to me to have life. — **John 5:39-40 (NIV)***

Jesus said to the Pharisees, "You diligently study the Scriptures" (John 5:39 NIV). I wonder why they did? Why do people ever choose to read the Bible? Of all our motivations, only one has staying power. Only one moves us beyond curiosity to study them diligently. Jesus put His finger on it: "You think that by them you possess eternal life" (John 5:39 NIV).

Not all Bible readers are Christians, but they are all on a quest. They are trying to find answers and a framework or philosophy large and deep enough for a life with meaning and staying power. They have been around long enough, read enough books, sat through enough lectures, and experienced enough to know that if the search is to end in satisfaction, it has to lead to "god" or "a god."

They may not be sure who or what "God" is, but history is filled with rumors that we can learn about Him and maybe even find Him if we read the Bible. So, they make the decision to begin the journey and search the Scriptures, hoping to find life. However, Jesus points out that honestly searching the scriptures will require diligence, because when one decides to study the Scriptures, trouble will begin almost immediately.

We are alternately bewildered, bored, inspired, enraged, and skeptical in no time. Scripture (if read seriously) will offend, challenge, and disappoint you on every level. It will be an affront to your intellect, your morality, your politics, and your religion. There simply is not one part of us that will not struggle as we interact with the Scriptures.

Scripture Will Offend

It starts with the first words: "In the beginning God created (Genesis 1:1 NIV). Your hopes may rise when you read those words. What better place to begin than the beginning? You may think that this first line is the introduction to a comprehensive explanation of how our universe with all of its complexities came to be. You may think that some "supreme being" has finally deigned to respond to your demands for answers.

But in the face of your curiosity and interrogation, all you hear is "God said…" over and over again. Are we really expected to settle for that?

It doesn't get better. If you are looking for exhaustive explanations for war, poverty, racism, hatred, and strife, Scripture will seem maddeningly simplistic. These challenges to your intellect will never stop. Scripture asks you to believe things that are hard to believe from its first page to its last.

If you are stubborn enough to press through that roadblock, prepare to be shocked and angered by the Scriptures. Beside your intellect, your sensibilities will also be offended. The Bible is not a storybook for church, and it is certainly not a manual in sensitivity training. Preachers or politicians with smooth hands and smoother answers did not write it to try to raise their approval ratings in the next poll. Nor was it written by religious motivational speakers trying to help us paint a happy face on life so we can pretend our way to success.

The Bible is an incredibly honest and irreligious book. It is stark and often barbaric. It smells of liquor and reeks of the smoke rising from burned-out cities and lives. Its pages are smudged with bloody fingerprints and stained with tears. It discriminates harshly. It draws bold lines. Who and what the Scriptures approve angers religious people, while who and what the Scriptures condemn angers secular people. The prayers that are recorded in the Bible were not uttered in sterile sanctuaries or chanted in secluded monasteries. Warriors screamed them as praise while they stood, sword in hand, over the slaughtered bodies of their enemies. Then there are the prayers that were choked out as sobs by men ready to sacrifice their children on altars, or whispered by women asking for blessings on their way to get men drunk and seduce them.

Scripture Will Challenge or Disappoint You

Not only will Scripture offend some, but it can also challenge or even disappoint. Make your way through the pages of the Bible and soon you find it drops you into the midst of a people and a culture you know nothing about.

You are left as a tourist who doesn't speak the language, without a guidebook. Scripture makes you visit the most uninteresting sights and take part in some of the most grating conversations. Page after page is filled with religious rules and family genealogies. Chapter after chapter is filled with dietary regulations and protocol for mysterious holy days of the Jewish people. It feels as if you are being forced to watch slide shows of your neighbor's trip to the last stamp-collecting convention for hours on end.

"You diligently study the Scriptures because you think that by them you possess eternal life" (John 5:39 NIV). The Pharisees read the Scriptures so carefully because they were trying to possess something. They were looking for a solution to their particular problem. They were not looking for a relationship; they were looking for a possession, a status, a standing. That is often what draws us to Scripture.

We don't read the Bible to learn about a person or develop a relationship. We approach the Bible as we do an Internet search engine. We want to type in our concern—"How to have a happy marriage," "Five Steps to Parenting Success," or "Three ways to make effective decisions"—and have the Bible spit back to us answers and programs for us to achieve our goals. We want solutions and answers, knowledge that serves us. We come looking to "possess," not to be engaged, challenged, and transformed.

The Bible wasn't commissioned and inspired for these purposes, and God refuses to pander. If we only seek out God's word for our own agenda or a quick fix to whatever problem we are facing, then we will miss God's plan for each of us and disappointment will follow.

So Why Bother?

If the Scriptures are like a foreign land in which we could be challenged or disappointed, then why would we seek to be in God's word? Because Jesus said, "These are the Scriptures that testify about me" (John 5:39 NIV). With all their violence, barbarism, and superstitions, as well as their humanity, these scriptures tell us about God better than any meticulously edited, perfectly paced, politically correct, "made for church" manual ever could.

They testify to Jesus. That is the primary function of Scripture. The Scriptures are not concerned with being nice. God did not commission the creation of Scripture so that we could have a religious book that comforts our souls and kisses our existential boo-boos. He inspired a real book, written in real life, so that we could get the real picture. He did not present Himself to us concisely and clearly, with chapter headings and a synopsis. Life doesn't come to us that way. Why should we expect God to come to us like that?

No, God allowed our understanding of Him to be worked out through real life and the superstitions of primitive and barbaric people. He allowed His truth to be roughly and violently handled by the warriors, chauvinists, bigots, and terrorists. He sent His full and final revelation, the person He had been writing about all those centuries to us, not as a full grown, awe-inspiring deity, but rather as a helpless baby born in the mess and stench of a manure-filled stall. He did not come to a fairy-tale world in a fairy-tale way. He dwelt among us, amid our selfishness, violence, fears, and sin. God always comes to us where we are, as we are, to tell us about Himself.

In Scripture we find God just as He has chosen to reveal Himself, one piece at a time. Scripture is His truth bursting out of the wineskins of our personal sinfulness and cultic rituals. The Bible is the honest record of our getting to know God painfully and slowly.

You may still refuse to come to Him—the Pharisees did. But if that is the case, at least make sure that you do so once you see the full picture. Don't stop the first time that you get angry or that it doesn't make sense. Do not allow the parodies of some preacher or the caricatures of some cynic to become an excuse for spiritual laziness. Don't reject your "idea" of God. Be diligent and see what He says about Himself. After all, He has paid you the compliment of revealing Himself to you in your world. Remember that, as you begin your search of the Scriptures, God is trying to make an introduction. He is trying to introduce Himself to you.

> The Bible is hundreds upon hundreds of voices all calling at once out of the past and clamoring for our attention ... the prophets shrill out their frustration, their rage, their holy hope and madness; the priests drone on and on about the dimensions and furniture of the temple; and the lawgivers spell out what to eat and what not to eat; and the historians list the kings, the battles, the tragic lessons of Israel history. And somewhere in the midst of them all one particular voice speaks out that is unlike any voice because it speaks so directly to the deepest privacy and longing and weariness of each of us that there are times when the centuries are blown away like mist, and it is as if we stand with no shelter of time at all between ourselves and the one who speaks our secret name. 'Come', the voice says. All of you, every last one. — **Frederick Buechner**[2]

In the end, that is where the Scriptures can lead you—where you really need and want to go.

But Jesus said that for all their diligent searching of the Scriptures, the Pharisees refused to come to Him (John 5:40). Somehow, amidst all the other voices, they missed the one voice they needed to hear. God waits patiently for us to come into His Word, just as He did with the Pharisees. The invitation is always there, but not everyone will respond.

Reading the Bible Is Never Enough

The bright red words "Bible Classes for All Ages" scrolled across a church's digital sign as I drove past. I wondered if the opportunity to attend Bible classes had caused any commuter's heart to race with hope and anticipation that morning. I wondered if the mother in a minivan on her way to a meeting at school to discuss her rebellious son found any hope in the offer. I wondered if it struck a chord with the small contractor in the pickup truck hoping to get at least enough work to buy some groceries this week, or the husband whose wife had just told him she was leaving him to be with another man, or the young couple with three children driving from a doctor's visit to a specialist because the wife was just diagnosed with cancer. Do you really think they just could not wait to get to a Bible class? Filling our minds with knowledge of Scripture is a good thing, but it is never enough. We have to hear the author's voice to receive the benefits intended when He commissioned the book.

Jesus Himself furnished the model for how the Scriptures are intended to impact our lives. At the outset of His ministry on earth, the Gospels record that Christ was led into the wilderness for forty days.

He ate nothing during those days, and at the end of them he was hungry.

*The devil said to him, "If you are the Son of God, tell this stone to become bread." — **Luke 4:2-3 (NIV)***

When Matthew told the story, he wrote that Jesus responded, "It is written: 'Man does not live on bread alone, but on every word that comes from the mouth of God" (Matthew 4:4 NIV).

Our most serious temptations arise from real needs. Nobody is tempted "in theory." Jesus had been fasting for forty days, so He was "hungry." He was *really* hungry. So naturally the devil came after that hunger first: "Prove you are God and make bread. You can kill two birds with one stone." It sounds so practical. It seems so innocent. It makes perfect sense. So do all temptations to take shortcuts to meet legitimate needs.

When you are very lonely, it makes perfect sense to stay in a relationship that is borderline abusive and convince yourself to overlook and rationalize the inexcusable. When you are struggling financially, it makes perfect sense to sell things you shouldn't sell and accept clients you shouldn't accept.

We can all put a "spin" on these actions. The needs are real, normal, and natural. The temptations we succumb to and the sins we commit most often are caused by our efforts to get legitimate needs met in illegitimate ways. We are trying to turn stones into bread, trying to feed our hearts with things not suited for that purpose. That temptation is the first and most common.

Jesus shows us how to respond: "It is written." There is no denying the critical role that knowledge of God's written word plays in our lives. Jesus does quote what is "written." The written Scriptures are a shield for our souls. If we are ignorant of what is written, we will be vulnerable prey for the enemy. Pay close attention to what the cited scripture says: "Man does not live on bread alone, but on every word that comes from the mouth of God" (Matthew 4:4 NIV).

Jesus is telling us about the words that come directly from the living God to our hearts. He is telling us that what will feed our soul and sustain our spirit in the day of struggle is the intimate relationship we have with the living God. A preacher named A. W. Tozer used to say that because the "Bible is the written word of God...it is confined and limited by the necessities of ink and paper." However, the voice of God, the living Word, is as free as the Sovereign God Himself.[3]

That is why Jesus told us, "The words I have spoken to you are spirit and they are life" (John 6:63 NIV). It is the Voice of God that makes the written Word so powerful. The Bible will never be a living book until we are convinced that God still speaks today. We will never have the vitality and strength to face and live abundantly in the real world, which seems so dead and impersonal at times, if we think we are equipped through diligent Bible studies that fill our heads with doctrine, but never open our ears to hear the Spirit whisper to us.

Understand that the devil always goes after a deeper need than what is obvious when he tempts us. He approached Christ with: "If you are the Son of God" (Luke 4:3 NIV). Out there alone, weary, and hungry, Jesus's real struggle wasn't the physical hunger but the temptation to question His connection with His Father. Does that sound familiar? I believe that as much as His knowledge of the Scriptures was a help to Jesus, even more was the fact that just a few weeks before, He had heard God say, "You are my Son. I love you. I am pleased with you" (see Mark 1:11). If He hadn't heard that in His heart, then I wonder if He would have been saved by what was in His head.

The final year before we were married, my wife and I lived ninety-two miles apart from one another. Ninety-two exactly. I know because I drove those miles every weekend to spend time with her. We were separated during the week, so we would often send each other letters. Those letters told me of her likes and dislikes. She wrote to me of her love for me. She told me about her dreams for our future together. I learned a lot about her. I had absolute confidence in what I was learning because her own hand wrote those letters directly from her own heart. As valuable as those letters were, how awkward and unfulfilling would it have been if I drove to her home each weekend, sat on the couch in her presence, unfolded the letters and read them to her, then folded them back up and said, "Thank you honey, it has been nice spending this time with you"?

But isn't that how we treat the living God with the written Word? The letters are certainly God's word to us. But the purpose of those words is to draw us to a personal encounter with the Living God, who longs to speak personal words to us—words about our loneliness, about our struggles, about our anger, selfishness, and confusion—so we can avoid trying to "squeeze bread from a rock" and really live.

We live by the words that proceed from the mouth of the Lord. If you want to live, then yes, read the

Scriptures, but then wait for the whisper. Get in the habit of saying, "Speak, Lord, Your servant is listening."

Chapter 2 Notes

CHAPTER THREE

Stop Trying to Pray

One day Jesus was praying in a certain place. When he finished, one of his disciples said to him, "Lord, teach us to pray, just as John taught his disciples."

He said to them, "When you pray, say:

'Father, Hallowed be your name, your kingdom come. Give us each day our daily bread. Forgive us our sins, for we also forgive everyone who sins against us. And lead us not into temptation.'

Then Jesus said to them, "Suppose you have a friend, and you go to him at midnight and say, 'Friend, lend me three loaves of bread; a friend of mine on a journey has come to me, and I have no food to offer him.' And suppose the one inside answers, 'Don't bother me. The door is already locked, and my children and I are in bed. I can't get up and give you anything.' I tell you, even though he will not get up and give you the bread because of friendship, yet because of your shameless audacity he will surely get up and give you as much as you need.

"So I say to you: Ask and it will be given to you; seek and you will find; knock and the door will be opened to you. For everyone who asks receives; the one who seeks finds; and to the one who knocks, the door will be opened.

"Which of you fathers, if your son asks for a fish, will give him a snake instead? Or if he asks for an egg, will give him a scorpion? If you then, though you are evil, know how to give good gifts to your children, how much more will your Father in heaven give the Holy Spirit to those who ask him!" — **Luke 11:1-13 (NIV)**

A young pastor was excited that the president of his alma mater accepted an invitation to come and speak at his church. The day arrived and the president spoke to a surprisingly good crowd. Everything went well. The relieved and grateful pastor headed home to enjoy Sunday dinner with the president as his guest of honor. His wife had prepared a wonderful meal and set the table with their finest china. As the family gathered around the table, the proud pastor asked his five-year-old son to say the blessing.

"But I don't know how to pray," the boy protested shyly.

The mother laughed uneasily and encouraged her son, "Oh, honey, just pray like you hear mommy pray."

The reluctant little boy folded his hands as the family and their guest of honor bowed their heads.

Then the boy shrieked, "Dear God, why did we invite all these people to dinner?"

Learning by Example

We learn life's most important lessons by observation. Faith is caught more than it is taught. Luke shares with us a case in point. Jesus and the disciples were enjoying some down time together in Bethany at the home of Lazarus. "One day Jesus was praying in a certain place. When he finished, one of his disciples said to him, 'Lord teach us to pray, just as John taught his disciples'" (Luke 11:1 NIV). I am so glad someone made that request. It shows me that even the disciples struggled with this issue of prayer, and it gives us a chance to hear how Jesus responded.

Most of us do struggle with prayer, and we aren't offered much that is helpful. Chuck Swindoll said it best:

> To be painfully honest with you, most of the stuff I have ever read or heard said about prayer has either left me under a ton-and-a-half truckload of guilt or wearied me with pious-sounding clichés and meaningless God-talk. Because I didn't spend two or three grueling hours a day on my knees as dear Dr. So-and-So did...or because I wasn't able to weave dozens of Scripture verses through my prayer...or because I had not been successful in moving mountains, I picked up the distinct impression that I was out to lunch when it came to this part of the Christian life.[4]

It's tragic really, because prayer should be one of the simplest and most natural acts of faith we engage in. Prayer usually is the first act of faith for human beings.

Sooner or later everybody prays. We may weep, mutter to ourselves, or try to explain it away in some sophisticated manner.

But we are praying. If we pray, we have to believe someone is listening; otherwise we are really crazy! If we pray, we are acting in faith.

The FedEx executive lost on a deserted island in the movie *Castaway* painted a face on a volleyball so he could have a friend named "Wilson" to talk with. We all talk when we are alone. Prayer is the faith that we are speaking with someone. Even though it comes naturally to us and we all do it, we still struggle with prayer. That is why hearing what Jesus has to say about it is critical and extremely helpful.

Prayer Should Be Simple and Personal

Jesus responded to the request by teaching them a simple prayer. We have come to know it as the Lord's Prayer, and the version Luke gives us is remarkably uncomplicated and unpretentious. It is all of thirty-seven words long and doesn't contain one "thee" or "thou," quote one scripture, or use any word beginning with the prefix "omni-" (omnipresent, omniscient, omnipotent, etc.). How can this be?

Of course, we shouldn't make the mistake of confusing "simple" with "shallow." The equation two plus two equals four is simple, but it is also absolute and expresses a profound truth. The disciples asked Jesus to teach them how to pray, and He didn't brush off the request as if it were unnecessary. He taught them and us how to pray. The implication is that there is a correct way for us to pray, and it can be taught. The Scriptures speak of prayer that is "powerful and effective" (James 5:16 NIV). If there is such a thing as prayer that is powerful and effective, then there is prayer that is weak and ineffective. This is a critical question, and Jesus takes it seriously. In fact, this is not the only time that Christ taught this approach to prayer.

Matthew records the time that He taught this same prayer model to a crowd and then followed up the teaching with these words: "And when you pray, do not be like the hypocrites…And when you pray, do not keep on babbling like pagans" (Matthew 6:5-7 NIV). This may seem obvious, but I am going to risk pointing it out to you. Jesus essentially said, "Don't pray like this. When you speak to God, don't do it like this." How stunning in our age of pluralism and political correctness that Jesus actually tells us there are types of prayers God would rather not hear! He mentioned specifically the prayers of hypocrites and pagans. In contrast, what does effective prayer look like?

Prayer is personal. That means that it is a meaningful conversation with a personal God. Jesus told us to pray, "Our Father." He didn't say that we should pray by clearing our minds and trying to become one with the universe. He didn't teach us how to chant a mantra that would help us unite with a life force or a great "over soul." He also didn't tell us to get in touch with the spark of divinity within each of our own hearts. He instructed us to address a personal God who is distinct from us but very deeply concerned for us. "Our Father" is a profound way to pray, and it is also the only effective way to pray.

Our church hosted a banquet for an organization in our city that teaches adults to read and earn a GED. Hundreds attended, and there was a lot of clean-up work to do afterward. I was trying to break down and put away an eight-foot-long table and knew I needed help. How would I get it? If I stood there and lifted my eyes up to the universe and sent out a positive thought that would yield me assistance, would that work? Instead, I decided to speak to a person who was nearby: "Hey, John, could you help me?" And he did.

Pagans engage in all sorts of weird babbling and crazy gyrations, hoping that someone will hear them. Christians look to their Father and ask: "Will you help me?" No other faith system or religion teaches you to approach God this way.

Prayer is also normal and natural. If pagans pray hoping that someone will hear them, then hypocrites pray hoping that someone will see them. Jesus said that "they love to pray standing in the synagogues and on the street corners to be seen by men" (Matthew 6:5 NIV). They are not concerned about the kingdom of God. They are concerned about their reputation and aware of others who are listening, so they work to come off as learned and deep in their prayers. They string together theological concepts and Scripture verses. They do it all in a very deep church voice.

Jesus takes all the fun out of prayer for this religious show-off. He comes along and teaches us to pray like this:

"Dear Father, I praise Your holy name. Lord, set this messed-up world right; do what You desire here among us the way You do in heaven! You know we need to eat, Lord, so we ask You to provide. You have been so good to forgive us, Lord; we need Your forgiveness. Remind us to be forgiving with others. You know, God, we can get messed up, so keep us safe from ourselves and the devil. You are in charge, You can do whatever You want, and You are awesome. Amen."

That is not an attempt on my part to be flip or funny. This is my attempt to show you that your prayers should be simple and personal. Prayer is talking with God about things that concern us, things that concern Him, and things that we can do together. It is simply sharing love, concerns, and needs with your Father. That is the nature of prayer.

Prayer Is Powerful

Immediately after Jesus gave them that simple pattern of prayer, He told them a story designed to show us that although prayer is simple, it is also extremely powerful (Luke 11:5-13 NIV).

The story was of a man who had an unexpected guest arrive at midnight. Customs of the time made hospitality an absolute requirement and lack thereof a terrible shame. But the man was unprepared, so he wound up pounding on his neighbor's locked door, begging for a few loaves of bread so he could fulfill his obligations and save his reputation. His understandably grouchy neighbor growled at him to get lost and let him and his family sleep, but the man was persistent and insistent— which paid off as he received the help he needed from his reluctant neighbor.

Jesus used the word *ask* over and over again in the story, and He had a reason for this redundancy. He wanted us to understand that prayer is not a religious activity. Prayer is a life-changing interaction. Jesus never taught us to do anything for the sake of pure ceremony. Christianity is a ruthlessly practical faith. Every activity of the Christian faith is designed to have some tangible impact on the life that we live, which is why it makes religious people nervous—even angry. Here are the practical truths about prayer:

Be careful for nothing; but in every thing by prayer and supplication with thanksgiving let your request be made known to God. — **Philippians 4:6 (KJV)**

Jesus said, "Until now you have not asked for anything in my name. Ask and you will receive, and your joy will be complete." — **John 16:24 (NIV)**

Jesus said that asking Him was the key to complete joy and deliverance from concern and anxiety. Not acting on this directive of the Lord is one of the greatest reasons for fatigue, failure, and struggle in our lives. There are dozens of truths that we can share about prayer, but this is a powerful one to begin with. File it away. God wants us to ask Him for things when we pray.

Ask God for help with things that concern you. Look again at how Jesus told the story: A man was caught unprepared by guests. The surprised host hadn't done any shopping. The grocery stores were all closed. So in desperation, he ran over to his neighbor's house and banged on the door. His irritated neighbor shouted through his locked door, "Get lost! Do you have any idea what time it is and when I have to get up for work? Idiot!" However, Jesus said that even if it is late, dark, cold, and inconvenient, if you are persistent, stubborn, desperate, and audacious enough and you beg long enough, he will get up and help you just to shut you up and get you to go home!

Does this mean that we have to beg and whine and pester God in order to get Him interested in doing things for us? Not at all. Jesus was teaching by contrast. What He wants us to see is the power of simply asking. Even in a sinful world full of selfish people, if you are bold and brazen enough to ask, you can often get people to do things for you. How much greater and more abundant will the response be when the One you are asking is your Father—the God who wants to bless you, who desires to help you, who stands ready and able to respond!

Here are two things we need to understand:

(1) God Is Concerned with What Concerns Us

Only needs and concerns that are extremely important to you personally are going to compel you to get up, get dressed, and go running to the neighbors at midnight. The nation's economy may be bad, but that doesn't get me up at midnight. But when I can't pay my mortgage, I will be up. The fact that a high percentage of marriages end in divorce won't make me lose sleep, but when my marriage is falling apart, I can't go to sleep.

God is interested in the stuff that keeps us awake at night. The Father wants us to ask Him about the things that cause us to pace the floors at midnight. What is breaking your heart? What is stealing your peace? What is snatching away your joy? That's what God wants you to ask Him about: "Cast all your anxiety on him because he cares for you" (1 Peter 5:7 NIV). Dallas Willard said this extremely well:

> Many people have found prayer impossible because they thought they should only pray for wonderful but remote needs they actually had little or no interest in or even knowledge of. Prayer simply dies from efforts to pray about "good things" that honestly do not matter to us. The way to get to meaningful prayer for those good things is to start by praying for what we are truly interested in. The circle of our interests will inevitably grow in the largeness of God's love.[5]

(2) God Alone Is Able

Jesus told the story in a very intentional way. A friend stopped by at midnight—midnight, for crying out loud! Who shows up needing a sandwich at midnight? Jesus knew that the picture He was painting was unusual and unlikely. He taught it this way to show us that we need to be communicating with God all the time because life happens all the time. Life is full of "midnight moments."

When a family member is rushed to the hospital and you have moments to decide whether to sign a DNR, it is midnight. When your spouse looks across the room at you and tells you they want a divorce, or when you receive a call from the police station telling you your child was arrested for drugs, it's midnight. When you lose your home, lose your job, or lose your hope, it's midnight in your world no matter what time it says on the clock.

No one is prepared for times like that. No one has their shelves stocked with snappy answers to crises like that. Since life tends to happen all the time, God is available to you all the time. When life's demands are unreasonable, its situations are intolerable, and every shelf in your heart is barren, the Father has the bread. "My God can supply all your needs according to his riches in glory!"

Since life happens all the time, ask all the time! Keep on asking, keep on seeking, keep on knocking. You cannot wear God out; you cannot exhaust His concern for you. You cannot use up His resources. If you ask, you will receive; if you seek, you will find; if you knock, God will open doors for you. God is able to handle those midnight problems. But prayer is powerful not only because we can ask God about what concerns us; we can also:

Trust God to Do What's Best for Us

"Which of you fathers, if your son asks for a fish, will give him a snake instead? Or if he asks for an egg, will give him a scorpion?" — **Luke 11:11-12 (NIV)**

"Which of you, if his son asks for bread, will give him a stone? Or if he asks for a fish, will give him a snake?" — **Matthew 7:9-10 (NIV)**

This is a series of questions that seem odd to our ears. The New Testament scholar William Barclay wrote of these verses, "In the region of Galilee, lime stones often were exactly the shape and color of bread…'snake' meant 'serpent or eel,' which was an unclean fish…a scorpion at rest with its tail rolled in might even resemble an egg."[6]

Jesus juxtaposed these objects to teach us that when you come to God with your needs, you can trust that He will give an answer that is healthy and blessed. You will not get some dangerous or destructive substitute handed to you. What a blessing such knowledge can be!

We all have a tendency to pursue artificial happiness. An affair can look and feel very much like love. Great success at business and the financial rewards can look like happiness. Popularity can resemble friendship. So we will often pursue things, clutch at things, and get involved in things that look like what we think we need and want, only to find out that they bring pain, brokenness, and guilt into our lives. Contrary to that, if we simply trust and ask God and wait for His answer, then He will bless us.

Pat strolled into the little sanctuary of our church in Ft. Lauderdale one Sunday. He had often been invited by a friend and had often refused. Pat stayed busy most weekends playing the drums for a Southern-fried rock band in local bars. He looked like a guy who played drums in bars on the weekend. But now he was in church, and he showed up for a few weeks before I began to learn why he had suddenly decided to give the church a try. Pat's wife was a drug addict and had recently run away with her dealer, leaving him to try to raise two young girls alone. He knew he needed God.

He and his girls continued to worship with us, and Pat began to display a real hunger for Jesus. Finally, he met Christ personally on a retreat with several other men from our church. He was full of excitement. He was at every Bible study. He asked hundreds of questions and invited several friends. But then I noticed that he started to miss some Sundays and that the shine of his enthusiasm had dimmed a bit. One Sunday after worship, he asked if we could step into my office and talk.

Pat slumped down into the chair at my desk and began to pour his heart out. He talked about how lonely he was and how difficult it was to raise the girls alone, especially now that his oldest was getting close to puberty. Then he told me that he had met a woman and begun to date her. He liked her. Then he looked at me and said, "Pastor, she wants us to move in together and I am really interested. What do you think?"

You have to understand. Pat was one of the nicest guys and most genuine souls I have ever pastored. We had prayed together often that God would assist him in finding a helpmate. I understood and sympathized deeply with his heart. Yet I swallowed hard and responded, "Pat, I feel your pain, I do. But you and I both know what the Bible says about adultery. This lady obviously doesn't share your faith, and as lonely as you are, as desperately as you need help, as your pastor and friend I want to urge you to not compromise or settle for this shortcut. I just have to believe that God will meet your needs in his time and in a much better way."

He nodded. I prayed. He left. I had no idea what Pat would do. The next week he showed up at church and told me that he had ended the relationship with his girlfriend. He wasn't smiling. But Pat stuck with his commitment.

I moved away from Ft. Lauderdale about a year later. One month after I had relocated, I received a phone call from Pat telling me that his ex-wife had called him. She had gone to a church service in South Carolina, and Jesus had saved her there. She had been growing in her faith and finally knew that she needed to call and ask him for his forgiveness. Now she was coming to Ft. Lauderdale to see him. Several months later, I drove down to Ft. Lauderdale and performed their marriage ceremony. One year later, they messaged me on Facebook that they would be having their first grandbaby. Seventeen years have gone by and the two of them still love the Lord and one another.

Life doesn't always work out all that neat and tidy. But here is what I know: If you trust God, if you ask for His answer and wait for His way, He will bless you— and "the blessing of the Lord makes us rich and he adds no shame to it."

Prayer Has One Primary Purpose

Why do we pray? Paul puts it this way: "...because we are God's children, God has sent forth his Spirit into our hearts crying, 'Abba, Father'" (Galatians 4:6). We pray because we have received a spirit of adoption that prompts us to cry out "Father."

Jesus ends His teaching with this promise: "...how much more will your Father in heaven give the Holy

Spirit to those who ask him!" (Luke 11:13). The Lord invites us to begin our relationship by asking Him for what we need, when we need it, over and over again and all the time. However, if you do that long enough and often enough, something will dawn on you—you will realize that all you really need is God Himself. All you need for your challenges and "midnight" moments is just God. Then what you long for and ask for will begin to change.

My father loves big cars. When I was young, he was always buying someone's used Mercury Marquis or Cadillac Sedan de Ville. An evening of entertainment for him was to find some winding country road, roll down all the windows, and cruise. He usually took all five of us kids along, but occasionally he would invite just one of us to ride with him. If Dad asked, "Jack, do you want to go for a ride with me?" I would respond by asking, "Can we stop and get a Coke and a candy bar on the way?" Most of the time the answer was yes. He was a good father and wanted me to ride along.

As time went by, I started to enjoy the rides as much as he did, and for the same reasons. I looked forward to the invitation. In fact, I stopped waiting. I started coming to him: "Hey Dad, you want to go for a ride?" Not because I wanted a Coke or a candy bar—I simply enjoyed being with my father, doing something he enjoyed, and talking about whatever came to mind. More than anything else, that time and our relationship were what I was asking for.

The greatest gift we get in prayer is God Himself. The more we respond to His invitation to ask Him for things, the greater our hunger for Him, for His Spirit grows in us. When we come into His presence, interact with Him, and depend on Him for the needs and desires of our lives, it won't be long before we realize what we really need, more than anything else, is more of God. We will begin asking for more of Him, and He will give Himself to us in greater ways than we could ever imagine through the Holy Spirit—when we make it a practice and priority to ask.

So stop trying to pray. Stop attempting to do it right. Give up on your efforts to be profound and selfless. Stop trying to impress people who aren't interested anyway. Stop trying to appease a god made in the image of religion. Just pray. Just speak with God respectfully, honestly, and expectantly.

You will be amazed at what happens.

Chapter 3 Notes

CHAPTER FOUR

You Don't Need More Faith

Jesus said to his disciples: "Things that cause people to stumble are bound to come, but woe to anyone through whom they come. It would be better for them to be thrown into the sea with a millstone tied around their neck than to cause one of these little ones to stumble. So watch yourselves. 'If your brother or sister sins against you, rebuke them; and if they repent, forgive them.'"

The apostles said to the Lord, "Increase our faith!"

He replied, "If you have faith as small as a mustard seed, you can say to this mulberry tree, 'Be uprooted and planted in the sea,' and it will obey you. Suppose one of you had a servant plowing or looking after the sheep. Will he say to the servant when he comes in from the field, 'Come along now and sit down to eat'? Won't he rather say, 'Prepare my supper, get yourself ready and wait on me while I eat and drink; after that you may eat and drink'?

"Will he thank the servant because he did what he was told to do?

*"So you also, when you have done everything you were told to do, should say, 'We are unworthy servants; we have only done our duty.'" — **Luke 17:1-10 (NIV)***

Take a minute and let your eyes roam through these verses to where Jesus says that if we have faith the size of a mustard seed, we could command a tree to be ripped up by the roots and cast into the sea and it would happen. A verse like this preaches really well in the fervent atmosphere of a revival service, but few of us ever experience any such phenomena in our daily lives.

Keep rewinding through the Scriptures and you will come to Jesus commanding you to forgive your brother even if he sins against you seven times in the same day. Jesus said *what*? Be honest, don't statements like that make you wonder what color the sky was in Jesus's world?

Of course, rather than express doubts, the disciples discreetly responded: "Lord, increase our faith!" That request sounds holy and sincere. We have prayed prayers like this ourselves. However, Jesus has little patience for it because it is a religious cop-out and reveals what has always been a fundamental misunderstanding of faith.

Faith Is Meant for Real Life

Jesus's opening premise is not subtle or nuanced. Our world is a desperate place where it will be tough to maintain a walk with God. M. Scott Peck wrote a book entitled *The Road Less Traveled*. I do not remember tons about it, but I will never forget the first line: "Life is difficult." In fact, that was the entire first paragraph. Then, in the next, he wrote: "This is a great truth because once we see it we can transcend it....Most of us will not embrace the truth that life is difficult. Instead we moan more or less incessantly about the enormity of our problems as if life is generally easy, as if life should be easy."[7]

He went on to write that if we can embrace the truth that life is difficult, then we learn to transcend the difficulty. I think he was spot on, and that is exactly the reality that Jesus was laying out here.

Bad things are bound to come; that's life. He said it in a very "matter of fact" way and He used an interesting word. He said that there will constantly be things that will trip you up or "cause you to stumble." All through the New Testament, our life of faith is depicted as a walk. We are told, "As you therefore have received Christ Jesus the Lord, so walk in Him" (Colossians 2:6 NKJV). And in this world, as you are trying to live for Christ, trying to walk the straight and narrow, things are going to come along that will trip you up and tempt you to get off track.

No two people reading this book are exactly the same, but there is one thing that is true of all of us: Every one of us has been hurt, disappointed, and disillusioned by life at some point. Jesus told us this was going to happen. The problem with the world is that it is full of people, and people are difficult. We do stupid things and behave selfishly. We offend and get offended. That reality—the real world—is the climate in which faith is meant to operate.

Faith is often seen as a tool that, if we can learn to manipulate it in the correct fashion, will cause problems and challenges to evaporate. Money will fall from the sky, disease will run from our bodies, bad neighbors will move to Montana, and irritating in-laws will lose their voices and directions to our house. Faith extricates us from the hard situations of life, or at the very least builds a bubble around us so that they do not touch our lives. But Jesus never promised us this. In fact, He said that we will experience offensive things.

We will be "sinned against." And Jesus got very specific. He didn't deal with injustice and the wrong in some general or theoretical way. He talked about when a "brother" sins against us. C. S. Lewis wrote, "Everyone says forgiveness is a lovely idea, until they have something to forgive."[8] We have no problem with forgiveness as long as Jesus is talking about some people "out there" who need to forgive other people "out there." But we become defensive when he looks at us and says, "you need to forgive your brother who sinned against you."

Peter once questioned Jesus about that very thing, "Lord, how many times shall I forgive my brother when he sins against me?" (Matthew 18:21). I promise you that Peter knew the "brother" he was asking about. Peter wasn't asking a doctrinal question. He was asking a personal question. A brother and a friend had hurt him, and he was trying to decide how to deal with it. That is when we really want and need to know. That is when we find out just how much good our faith really is. All of us will have our faith tested in this manner.

Sometimes we will be sinned against over and over again by the same people. People will come to us and tell us they are sorry and then turn around and do the same hurtful stuff again. Any child of an alcoholic understands that scenario. Anyone who was abused understands that long after the abuser is gone and cannot apologize, the memories show up to torment us over and over again. Anyone who grew up in a racist culture resonates with these words. People of faith in a world that is increasingly hostile to faith feel these words.

Then Jesus continued by saying something really odd: "So watch yourselves" (Luke 17:3 NIV). He didn't say, "Protect yourselves," or "Defend your rights." He didn't say, "Watch out for those people." He turned the focus onto us. Jesus knew that when we are hurt and offended, we are in a very dangerous position.

Anger always follows hurt. Revenge is the first instinct of anger. If we have been offended, then we will want to offend someone right back! So before long, the world is full of people offending and being offended. Sadly, this captures the climate of public life in America today.

The problem for Christ followers is that when this world looks at people who claim to have faith, but have become bitter, angry, unforgiving, and militant, it is cause for them to stumble. When we use the offenses that Jesus promised us we would experience as justification to return offense, sarcasm, scorn, lies, and anger, it scandalizes the gospel. It trips people up. Jesus told us that our concern for the gospel, for the name of Christ, and for the salvation of the lost has to outweigh our desire to get even.

To some degree, we have to be willing to be offended over and over again rather than give offense even once.

Faith is what gives you the power to live this way. However, in order to experience it, you have to come to grips with this next fact:

You Already Have All the Faith You Need

You have to love the honesty of Scripture. The disciples hear Jesus say these things and they respond, "Increase our faith!" What Jesus just said sounded impossible and, honestly, ridiculous. He just said that if we are hurt by someone seven times in the same day, we must forgive them every time. I understand the symbolism and the hyperbole that Christ employed here, but the point remains. He was telling us that we must always forgive, all the time, no exceptions. Most of us aren't sure we believe that is possible. Even if it is, most of us are not sure we want to do it. I mean, we have names for people who get hustled over and over by the same person: "Push-over, chump, loser." Oh, and "BROKE!" This is one of those moments when we are tempted to relegate our faith to theoretical discussions within a small group: "Well, that is a nice ideal for a perfect world."

But then we look at Jesus, and He is serious! He means for us to do this in the real world. The disciples didn't want to be rebellious, so they exclaimed: "Increase our faith!" That sounds very pious and sincere, but we can't use the same escape hatch every time we come up against one of these challenging commands of Christ:

"Lord, give me more faith to love my neighbor."

"Give me faith to let go of the money you told me to give."

"Give me the faith to stick with my marriage."

"Give me the faith to end this relationship."

"Give me the faith to speak up for the person I see being mistreated."

It sounds like you are being sincere when you are truly being rebellious. You are saying that God has not given you sufficient resources to do what He is commanding you to do. Jesus never has time for that sort of religious posturing. "He replied, 'If you have faith as small as a mustard seed, you can say to this mulberry tree, 'Be uprooted and planted in the sea,' and it will obey you" (Luke 17:6 NIV).

Invoking the mustard seed was a rabbinical way of saying "the smallest amount possible." Jesus was telling them and us that if you have the smallest amount of faith, you can do what He tells you to do. When it comes to faith, our problem is not the quantity of our faith, but the quality of our faith. What is standing between us and miracles is not what we are able to believe, but what we aren't willing to do.

Obedience Is the Issue

Christ followed up His declaration about faith with an interesting story about a servant and his master. He told his disciples to put themselves in the position of the master, and described the situation: The servant works in the field all day, and dinner time comes. If you are the master, do you look at the servant and say, "Man, you look like you had it rough. Have a seat and let me prepare dinner tonight"? Not one of them would do that. Yes the work is hard; yes the servant may be tired, but that is his job. This is the nature of the relationship. The servant remains obedient and active, and he does what he is responsible to do for his master.

The point is that many of us never see God move mulberry trees, let alone mountains, because we are under the impression that it is supposed to be easy. When we are facing a mountain of debt, we think that faith is about introducing prosperity to our finances because we believe these things will work, not living on a budget and obeying the commands of God about stewardship. When we have roots of bitterness deeply twined around our hearts in our marriages, we think we can make a quick trip to an altar or a weekend retreat and faith will zap us with a secret "forgiveness ray." But faith would go to counseling and make a commitment to keep coming home every day, even when you are tired and it is no fun and the "thrill is gone." Faith would do this, trusting that the Master would eventually uproot that anger and hurt and replace it with renewed love.

We are always looking to God when we hear His commands and read His promises, and we ask Him to give us "more." The reality is, He has given us all we need; we simply have to do what He told us to do. That is putting faith in action. Living that way uproots mulberry trees and moves mountains in our lives.

You see, faith isn't a button that you use to get God to arrange life the way you want it to work. Faith is the power that enables you to live life the way the Master tells you to live it. Jesus is telling us this: "When you have faith to do what I say, to live how I tell you to live…

"…even when it seems unreasonable…

"…even when it seems unfair…

"…even when you are tired, unrewarded, and unnoticed…

"When you have that sort of faith, that quality of faith, you will do things you never believed you were capable of doing."

That is why Jesus responded to their desperate plea for more faith with the promise that faith as small as a grain of mustard seed can uproot a mulberry tree.

Really think for a moment about what is being said here. Jesus is telling you that if you live in faith, if you take even small actions of obedience, things that have been deeply rooted in your life can be uprooted and cast out. Deeply rooted bitterness, deeply rooted family issues, addictions, financial struggles, and guilt—stuff that has wrapped around your heart and borne the fruit of anger and despair and sleepless nights—can be cast out of your life by just a little bit of faith.

If we have just enough faith to do what we are told, suddenly we will begin to see our lives change. We will begin to see sin uprooted and cast out of our lives. Faith is a living seed throbbing with life-changing potential, but it needs to be planted in the soil of an obedient heart. A little faith plus a lot of obedience leads to miracles.

God has already given us all that we need to experience the miraculous.

Chapter 4 Notes

_____

_____

_____

_____

_____

_____

_____

_____

_____

_____

_____

_____

_____

_____

_____

_____

_____

_____

_____

_____

_____

_____

_____

_____

CHAPTER FIVE

How to Miss God's Will for Your Life

(All the people, even the tax collectors, when they heard Jesus' words, acknowledged that God's way was right, because they had been baptized by John. But the Pharisees and the experts in the law rejected God's purpose for themselves, because they had not been baptized by John.)

Jesus went on to say, "To what, then, can I compare the people of this generation? What are they like? They are like children sitting in the marketplace and calling out to each other:

" 'We played the pipe for you, and you did not dance; we sang a dirge, and you did not cry.'

"For John the Baptist came neither eating bread nor drinking wine, and you say, 'He has a demon.' The Son of Man came eating and drinking, and you say, 'Here is a glutton and a drunkard, a friend of tax collectors and sinners.' But wisdom is proved right by all her children."
— Luke 7:29-35 (NIV)

I was reading this passage of Scripture at 6 a.m. I know that sounds holy, but the truth is I was groggy and working harder at gulping down my first cup of coffee than at reading. I am not sure even God wants to talk to me before I have had coffee. Still, sleepy or not, I was reading and God did speak with me when I read this verse: "But the Pharisees and experts in the law rejected God's purpose for themselves."

That line woke me up. It wasn't part of the story. Luke wrote this as a parenthetical explanation for the response to and behavior of people toward Jesus. But his explanation *explains almost everything*!

Our Purpose Affirms One of Our Greatest Hopes

God has a purpose for each of us. There are no "accidental tourists" in this universe. In all of history, God has never looked at one baby being born and said, "oops."

We may live for many years unacquainted with our innate desire for purpose, but it is waiting to introduce itself. G. K. Chesterton called it "a profound emotion always present and subconscious; that this world of ours has some purpose; and if there is a purpose, there is a person. I had always felt life first as a story: and if there is a story there is a story-teller."[9] His hunch, and ours, is right. God has a purpose for us.

However, the same line portrays one of our greatest fears. The fear that we could sleepwalk through our days, failing to ever find the reason for which we were created.

In this encounter, Luke records that the Pharisees "rejected God's purpose for themselves." In the years I have spent in ministry, I have been asked to speak with people about career choices, car purchases, family planning, medical treatment, parenting methods, budgeting, their choice of a spouse, and their choice of schools. That is the short list.

The questions are phrased to me in dozens of ways, but the real concern behind the majority of those counseling sessions is: "How we can know God's purpose?" I am trying to help them deal with the nagging fear that they may have missed it. It is good for us to fear that. Missing our divine purpose would be a great tragedy. One writer describes the possibility:

> It would be better to never have been born. The moment you've been waiting for, the end for which you were created...flies without you. The cares of the world are no excuse ... Whatever the great human enterprise currently at hand, the point is God's purpose. Seeking the Kingdom is the critical thing. Keep your eyes open or you might as well be dead. You already are. — **Virginia Stem Owens**

Everyone wrestles with this fear. In fact, John the Baptist wrestled with this issue. Herod had put John into prison for preaching against his immoral lifestyle, which John did to prepare the people of Israel for the coming of their Messiah. He had been so committed, zealous, and willing to suffer this persecution because he was convinced that Jesus was this Messiah and that the Kingdom was at hand. Now, sitting in a cell, doubts began to creep into his mind. Cracks began to appear in his faith. So John sent some of his disciples to Jesus with a question: "Are you the one who is to come, or should we expect someone else?" (Luke 7:20 NIV). That was John's way of asking, "Did I miss God's purpose? Did I do the right thing, or am I rotting in prison for a complete mistake?"

If the fear is that common and the possibility is that real, then it is something we should consider. How does it happen? What is it that causes us to miss God's purpose? I am not sure that there is an exhaustive answer to that question, but there is one fact that is hidden in this story that should serve as some measure of comfort to those who have the concern:

Missing God's Purpose Is a Choice

Luke tells us that these people "rejected" God's purpose. This term indicates a deliberate and willful decision. It isn't like they woke up one day and were suddenly shocked by what they had done. We cannot simply "miss" God's purpose. That is a misleading piece of religious jargon we need to do away with. It makes living as a Christ follower feel like a heavenly game of chance, as if God has His perfect plan hidden behind a curtain and we have to try and guess which one. But if we guess wrong, we will be eternally stuck with the consequences of our mistake.

"I really want to find the person God wants me to marry," a young lady whispered to me at the altar one Sunday morning. She had made her way to kneel there and now she was fighting to hold back anxious tears. We prayed and talked even after the service had been dismissed. I finally told her that the real problem she had was not a lack of a fiancé, but a lack of trust in the goodness of God. She spoke as if she really believed that God had picked out a perfect Prince Charming for her, but had hidden him and was forcing her to work her way through a stack of losers and abusers in order to find him. She was paralyzed by the fear that if she made a mistake, God would leave her stuck in endless marital hell with "Bubba" and his hound dogs.

God does not play with us like that. I am convinced that our God is a forgiving God who will not perpetually punish us for mistakes. In fact, even when we mess up and misstep, He can redeem our mistakes and failures and weave them into the perfect pattern He is making of our lives. I am also confident of this: God wants to reveal His will for us. He wants us to live in the center of His good plans and purposes. These people did not "miss" God's purpose: They "rejected" it.

If our concern is to be certain that we are living in God's purpose, we need to spend less time trying to see providential clues in our circumstances and more time gauging the condition of our day-to-day walk and our hearts. I do not think that rejection of God's purpose ever boils down to one decision. Rather, I think we reach the point of final rejection through a lifetime of small disobediences. We get in the habit of rejecting God. We are not faithful in little things. We do not live in obedience to the things that He has clearly revealed to us in his Word, and so we can't expect to hear or respond when He tries to move us into the center of His specific will for our lives. So if you really want to make a mess of your life, what does it take?

Being Full of Stubborn Pride

In commenting on how various groups responded to Jesus, Luke writes that one group "acknowledged that God's way was right because they had been baptized by John" while the other "rejected God's purposes for themselves because they had not been baptized by John." In other words, their ability to perceive and submit to God's will was tied to how they had responded to John's invitation to baptism. The Scriptures say that John came "preaching a baptism of repentance for the forgiveness of sins" (Luke 3:3 NIV). This means that John baptized you because you had acknowledged that you were a sinner and needed forgiveness. You admitted that your life needed to turn around. In submitting to baptism, you were stating that you were willing to give up all your plans and ideas and submit to God's truth and the leadership of the Holy Spirit. The prerequisite for being able to find God's plan is a heart already prepared to live God's plan.

Most people in our world are not willing to live on those terms. We turn to God for repairs, not for marching orders. We are not looking for God to tell us what He wants for our lives; we are asking Him to bless the desires we have for our own lives. We would like God to serve as an advisor, showing us the best ways to accomplish our goals, but we are not looking for Him to run our lives. So He won't.

God will not bother to reveal His purposes if we are not disposed to pursue them. The prerequisite for living in God's purposes is the humble acknowledgment that His ways are best for us. It requires a supernaturally granted humility that admits our plans are too small, too selfish, and too sinful. It demands the acceptance of the fact that whatever God doesn't run, we will ruin.

Can I suggest that one of the reasons you may be struggling to perceive the will of God for your life is that you have been unwilling to admit or confess that you have made a mess of things by pursuing your own agenda? Even if you are not sure that this confession is true yet, or if you are struggling, wouldn't it be a good place to begin? Simply get on your knees, open your heart, and honestly ask God to show you if there is any area of your life where you have refused to be obedient or just refused to listen. If you're willing to do that and are prepared to respond with true repentance, I promise you will begin to make real headway. Our own stubborn pride often stands in our way.

Then Jesus uses some words that point out another reason we struggle with finding God's will:

Being Unreasonable and Selfish

> Jesus went on to say, "To what, then, can I compare the people of this generation? What are they like? They are like children sitting in the marketplace and calling out to each other:
>
> "'We played the pipe for you, and you did not dance; we sang a dirge, and you did not cry.'" — **Luke 7:31-33 (NIV)**

There are children, and then there are spoiled, snot-nosed brat children. Jesus says our problem is that we live like the second type of children. I have raised three children. I have endured my share of sleep-overs and parties. If you want to learn something about human nature, just watch children play. When children play, they are practicing to become adults. So they pretend to do things grownups do. They play "house" or "school" or "army." They will get along well for a while, but if you have kids together for any length of time play-acting at life, there will soon be fight over one group not "doing it right." Thank goodness we outgrow that as we mature.

In Jesus's era, two of the biggest events that could happen where the people to whom Jesus was speaking lived were a wedding or a funeral. Everybody showed up for these events, including the kids. So it would only be natural that the kids would learn to play "wedding" or "funeral" together. They would imitate what they saw there: At a wedding you danced and at a funeral you dirged. I bet you that there was a group of kids close by playing in exactly the way Jesus was describing. They were trying to act like grownups, but they couldn't because one group wanted to play wedding and dance and the other group wanted to play funeral and dirge. Naturally, a fight would have broken out with one group yelling, "We can't have any fun because you guys won't dance!"

The other group, just as stubborn and just frustrated, would have screamed back, "We could all have fun if you would do what we want and dirge!"

Everybody wanted it his or her way, and nobody was willing to do it anyone else's way, so the result was that nobody got to have any fun. There was no dancing, no dirging, no nothing.

Every parent has refereed this type of altercation. And while we are smiling and nodding our heads, Jesus sticks the knife in us. That is a description of the "children of this generation." He meant you and I. We miss God's purpose because we want Him to play our game by our rules and we are notoriously fickle. Nothing will make us happy while we live with this selfish approach to life. When God strikes up the band for a dance, we want to sing a dirge, and when God sends some sorrow, we rail at him because we never get to dance. We want things to happen the way we want it—when we want it.

Being Impatient

Jesus finished His interaction by saying this: "John was a teetotaler and kept all the rules and you called him a possessed fanatic. I came and enjoyed all your parties and you called me a drunk and playboy" (Luke 7:33-34, paraphrased).

When you are pursuing God's will, don't stand around waiting for affirmation. No matter what the Lord tells you to do, there will be people who do not understand and who will find fault. They will call you a "religious fanatic" for some things and a "liberal heretic" for others. Following God will turn you into an equal-opportunity offender. Both political parties, every special interest group, and every denomination will have a reason to be upset.

So sticking with it is imperative. Jesus ended by saying that "wisdom is proved right by all her children" (Luke 7:35 NIV). In fact, it may take a whole new generation before your obedience pays off. If you need the approval and applause of your peer group, your family, or society in general, you will turn away. If you need to see results fast and you are easily discouraged, you will quit.

You will walk out on a marriage in year seven, when "the thrill is gone," and miss year twenty-eight and the opportunity to dance at a child's wedding with the "soul-mate" God has used life to craft for you. You will hand in your resignation in year three of a ministry and miss the breakthrough that was planned for year ten, or miss mentoring the world-changer who happens to be getting their diaper changed in the nursery this week.

If you want to reject God's will, these are my recommendations: Be prideful, be selfish, and be impatient. Those kinds of behavior seem to be doing a good job of ruining most lives.

But if you want to live in His will, just wake up each morning and humbly ask Him if you can walk with Him another day. Our God is a good God, and I have learned that He welcomes the company.

Chapter 5 Notes

_____

_____

_____

_____

_____

_____

_____

_____

_____

_____

_____

_____

_____

_____

_____

_____

_____

_____

_____

_____

_____

_____

CHAPTER SIX

Your Soul Mate Doesn't Exist

Some Pharisees came to him to test him. They asked, "Is it lawful for a man to divorce his wife for any and every reason?"

*"Haven't you read," he replied, "that at the beginning the Creator 'made them male and female'' and said, 'For this reason a man will leave his father and mother and be united to his wife, and the two will become one flesh'? So they are no longer two, but one flesh. Therefore what God has joined together, let no one separate." — **Matthew 19:3-6 (NIV)***

An article in *The Huffington Post* gave ten crazy reasons people filed for divorce.[10] I couldn't help myself, so I read some of the reasons:

- There was a Japanese woman who divorced her husband after she found out that he didn't like the Disney movie *Frozen*. In court, she said to him, "If you can't understand what makes this movie great, there's something wrong with you as a human being." All I could think was, "Somebody needs to tell her to 'Let it go!'"

- A Saudi woman filed for divorce because her husband had nicknamed her "Guantanamo" on his cellphone. She found out when she called him and realized that he had left his phone at home.

- Then there was the German woman who divorced her husband of fifteen years "because she couldn't stand his constant cleaning." One day he crossed the line. He actually "tore down a wall in their home because it was too dirty."

There were others that were just as silly and bizarre, but after I read the article, it occurred to me that we rarely understand the real causes behind the disintegration of most marriages. We think marriages end because the husband had an affair, or the wife is a closet alcoholic, or one of them gambled secretly and lost a ton of money, or one of them roots for the New England Patriots (that would be mine). But those events, as awful as they are, are usually just the final implosion of the relationship. Those huge hurts often come because of little irritations we do not deal with earlier.

One of the most heartbreaking things I have experienced in ministry begins with witnessing people stand in front of me at wedding ceremonies promising to "love, honor, and cherish" each other. In that moment it is obvious that they mean every word. They are in love.

However, after a few years have gone by, I often find myself sitting with the same couple in sessions full of animosity, anger, and mistrust. I ask the same question that so many others have: What causes that? How can two people who were so desperately in love now desperately want to get away from one another?

There is a book of poetry in the Old Testament entitled "The Song of Songs." It is an extended love song or poem between a young man and woman. King Solomon is traditionally credited as the author of the book. By Old Testament standards, it is racy stuff.

Get a load of how the young man in the poem speaks to the woman he is pursuing:

> *How beautiful you are, my darling! Oh, how beautiful! Your eyes behind your veil are doves. Your hair is like a flock of goats descending from the hills of Gilead. Your teeth are like a flock of sheep just shorn, coming up from the washing. Each has its twin; not one of them is alone. Your lips are like a scarlet ribbon; your mouth is lovely. Your temples behind your veil are like the halves of a pomegranate. Your neck is like the tower of David, built with courses of stone; on it hang a thousand shields, all of them shields of warriors. Your breasts are like two fawns, like twin fawns of a gazelle that browse among the lilies. Until the day breaks and the shadows flee, I will go to the mountain of myrrh and to the hill of incense. You are altogether beautiful, my darling; there is no flaw in you.* — **Song of Solomon 4:1-7 (NIV)**

I am not sure I know what all that means, but *VA-VA-VA VOOOM*! This guy is pitching some major woo. The book goes on like that. It is full of this passionate exchange of thoughts and emotions. The man speaks first, then the woman speaks about how deeply in love they are with one another. They include a metaphor and lots of similes, referring to their love as a rich and vibrant vineyard. Then in the middle of all their passionate talk, there is this line: "Catch for us the foxes, the little foxes that ruin the vineyards, our vineyards that are in bloom" (Song of Songs 2:15 NIV). Now I could get us bogged down in a lot of exegesis here, but I am going to cut to the chase. When it comes to the relationship between a husband and wife, it's the "little foxes," the little things, that lead to the big failures.

I listened to a pastor from Nashville, Tennessee named Pete Wilson preach a whole series of messages on that truth, which he entitled "Five Things That Destroy Relationships." His list of relationship killers included unforgiveness, secrets, leftovers, and leaving God out. All of the messages were biblical and insightful, but the one that seemed the most critical to me was the very first one he mentioned: the expectations we carry into our marriages.

As he shared his thoughts, Wilson caused me to remember my wedding day. I was married on what turned out to be the hottest day of the summer that year. The church was an old building without air conditioning and we had a large crowd. Since it was 1986, I had to dress in the obligatory white tuxedo. That wasn't bad enough—my wife decided that our wedding colors would be silver and "daphne rose." I learned that "daphne rose" was just a fancy way of saying "pink." So I got to stand before friends and family, on a day that would be forever immortalized by photographers, in a white tuxedo with a pink cummerbund. I looked like a gay marshmallow.

We don't all have such vivid memories of what we actually wore on our wedding day, but Pastor Wilson pointed out that along with the clothes we wore, which all could see, we were also wearing something none could see. We were all wearing an invisible backpack full of expectations we had for our relationship. When we slipped the rings on one another's finger, we also shifted that backpack of invisible and unspoken expectations onto our husband or wife to carry. "In other words," Wilson preached, "I said, 'I do' because I thought 'you would.'" That transaction becomes the source of most of the crises we will experience in our lives together.

Our Expectations Are Not Biblical

Who came to Jesus with the question of when it was acceptable to get a divorce? Pharisees! That is scandalous because they were the most demanding, zealous, and fastidious of all the religious sects of Judaism. They were thorough in their knowledge and serious in their observation of the law. Jesus said of them that they searched the Scriptures diligently in order to find life **(John 5:44).** They fought over the interpretation and application of every letter in the Law of Moses. Still, here they are asking Jesus about marriage, and what do they want to discuss? When it's okay to get a divorce.

I have had people ask me questions on this exact topic many times. Unlike the Pharisees who approached Jesus with ulterior motives, most of the time when people ask me this question, they are asking through tears. In those moments I always try to show them grace, but in my mind, there is always the thought: "Now is not the time to begin asking what God's will for your marriage is." People only start wanting to ask about God's will when they reach a crisis point. That is when we come to get a problem fixed or to find out how to get out of the mess we have created. Or we come to get God's stamp of approval on decisions we have already made and opinions we already hold.

We would have a lot less pain if we would come to Jesus before we got married instead of running to him after we have nearly ruined our marriage. If people would ask, "What is the purpose of marriage, and what type of person should I marry?" first, they would have to ask, "Can I get a divorce?" a lot less often!

But the biggest problem is where the Pharisees were getting their expectations and standards for the decisions they were making about marriage. After Jesus responded to their question about divorce, they argued with Him: "Why then, did Moses command that a man give his wife a certificate of divorce and send her away?" (Matthew 19:7 NIV). There is much that can be said about this verse, but the thought I want to emphasize here is that these men were setting their standards and making their decisions about marriage based upon Moses, not upon God's plan and purpose. That may shock you, but I am sure it shocked the Pharisees when Jesus said, "Moses permitted you to divorce your wives because your hearts were hard. But it was not this way from the beginning" (Matthew 19:8 NIV). The Pharisees' primary problem was the same one we have today—our approach to and expectations concerning marriage are not in line with God's.

In their devotional *Love Talk*, Les and Leslie Parrott wrote about an unusual bicycle race conducted in a village in India. It was unusual because the object of the race was to go the shortest distance possible within a specified time. At the start of the race, everyone set their bikes up at the starting line. When the gun sounded, the contestants would try to move the least—the shortest distance. When the time was up, the person who had gone the farthest was the loser; the person closest to the starting line was the winner.[11]

What if you show up to that race and don't understand the rules? When the gun sounds, you take off like lightning and pedal for all you are worth. After a few moments, sweating and out of breath, you look around and believe you are blowing the competition away. You assume you are on your way to winning when in reality you are on your way to losing, all because you don't understand the rules or the expectations. That is the reason so many people experience disappointment and pain in marriage. We enter the relationship with ideas that are not from the God who created marriage.

Everything You Have Been Taught Is Probably Wrong

God's plan and approach to marriage is probably the opposite of what you have been taught. It always has been! Jesus responded to the Pharisees' question by quoting to them from the creation narrative in Genesis 2:24-25, which is the first time marriage is mentioned in Scripture and the first description of what God intends to see happen when a man and woman become husband and wife. Theologians call this a "passage of primary reference," meaning that if you want to understand what God intended when He instituted marriage, this is the verse against which you measure all the other references to marriage.

But this clashed with how people were approaching marriage in the days Jesus walked the earth. When you look at the verse, who leaves? Who gives up home and family? The man does. Yet that never happened. God said the man will leave his family and his home to be united to his wife, but from the outset we humans did exactly the opposite. In every culture, even among God's chosen, when marriages were arranged, the wife left her home, her family, and her life to be with the husband. We never did it the way God told us to do it! Now you may be thinking, "That was a long time ago. Women aren't treated like that anymore. The situation has changed." Yes, but the foundational problem remains. We still enter marriage with the wrong expectations.

I perform a lot of weddings and almost always require the couples for whom I do this to spend time with me in some premarital preparation meetings. In the first session I will always begin with the same question. I ask, "Why do you want to marry Bob?" or "Why do you want to marry Sally?" There is one answer they cannot give me. They cannot answer, "Because I love him/her." I have heard hundreds of responses, but they fall into some predictable categories: "Marriage will cure my loneliness. Marriage is the 'next logical step.' Marriage will make me a better, or happier, or more fulfilled person." None of these are the correct reasons or purposes for marriage.

God told us what He had in mind for marriage, and Jesus reminded us that His purpose for marriage was, "For this reason…the two will become one flesh."

The True Nature of Marriage

Jesus said that when a man and a woman make a promise to one another, God hears and does something. You are no longer two, but He makes you one. That is not religious jargon, Jesus is telling us that this actually happens. Something real and profound takes place in the heavens and in your heart. Jesus says that in marriage a man will "be united to his wife."

The word "united" means "stuck like glue."

Several years ago, Tom Cruise made the movie *Vanilla Sky*. In it, a slightly deranged woman with whom he had a casual sexual encounter is stalking him. She finally manages to trap him in a car and is driving recklessly while screaming at him about how heartbroken she was when he jilted her. In the midst of her craziness however, the woman utters this incredible line: "Don't you know that when you sleep with someone, your body makes a promise even if you don't?" She may have been crazy, but she was right about that.

This happens whether we understand it or not. We make a promise in marriage and in sharing the marital bed. The promise is, "I'm with you. I will stick with you through diapers and degrees, mortgages and menopause, mid-life and meltdowns, for richer or poorer, in sickness and in health, until death do us part." We seal that covenant sexually and with sharing of deep intimacy and vulnerability. Something real happens.

When you break this covenant, there will be real suffering—not just for you, but also for others who will suffer collaterally. Jesus pointed this out when He said that the selfish decision of the Pharisees "caused" the wives to commit adultery (Matthew 19:9) People who have no control over the choices they make still suffer because of the breaking of covenant. If you are a believer at all, if you take the word of Jesus seriously at all, then you have to understand that every time you break a promise, a little more of the fabric of our universe unravels. Because marriage is a real covenant before God.

But then we must also understand that marriage is a real and human process. Jesus said that they "become one." "Become" is a word of process. It doesn't happen overnight: It happens over years.

"The two shall become one" sounds so romantic, doesn't it? Don't you just hear it and think, "Oh, that is lovely, that is so beautiful—two become one. I have goose pimples"? Well, snap out of it! This isn't romantic; this is real, and it is hard. You aren't ready for it. Nobody is ready for what you are getting into when you say "I do," and by the time you figure it out, you're already committed! That's why they make you promise on the front end of a marriage; they make you start off by saying "I promise for better and for worse." I guarantee there will be both. Some of it is going to be better than you expected, and some of it is going to be worse. Marriage is going to both exceed and frustrate your expectations.

I met with a distraught woman who was considering leaving her husband of eight years. She shared a few frustrations that didn't seem to amount to a lot, and I think saying them out loud to a preacher forced her to the realization that they weren't all that serious. Finally, exasperated, she said, "He's not the man I thought he was when I married him." I responded, "Yeah...so?"

I know that wasn't gentle and pastoral, but I want to let you in on something: no one is who you think they are when you marry them. Every Prince Charming eventually turns into a bullfrog. Guys, I am warning you, every super-fine woman eventually takes off her makeup and comes to bed in sweat pants. I know that you watched your parents and said to yourself, "We will never act like that. We will never lose the fire. I am going to marry my 'soul mate.'" But this leads me to share with you the radical thing Jesus implied about marriage in His words:

Your Soul Mate Doesn't Exist

I was lying on my couch, stuffing myself with Cool Ranch Doritos the first time I saw a commercial for eHarmony. You may know that eHarmony is a Christian-oriented dating site that promises to match people up based on "seventy-nine dimensions of deep compatibility." Seventy-nine! I nearly choked on my Doritos. For one, I have yet to meet a man who has seventy dimensions! Ladies, please take it from a man: We do not have seventy-nine dimensions. I am convinced there are some men who aren't even three-dimensional. If you try to connect with us on that many levels, you are just going to get frustrated and make us mad. But I digress. Here is the real concern:

What that commercial is selling is the idea that "becoming one" could be made simple—that we can boil it down to some tests and programs, and, if we follow them faithfully, we would be guaranteed marital success. There is the implied idea that some recipe or formula exists that will help us find "the one," the person with the exact chromosomal connections and chemical mixtures to be our soul mate. If God created such a person (as some of us believe) and it is our job to find them, then eHarmony is a great tool in that search.

However, remember Jesus said you "become one." That is not a word of discovery; it is a word of process. You don't discover and marry your "soul mate," you create your soul mate by being married to someone and loving them for a long time. You fight and you forgive. You mess up, get up, and move on. You have kids, change diapers, pay bills, and clean up messes. You fight some more and forgive some more. You don't start out as soul mates; you "become." "That is why a man leaves his father and mother and is united to his wife, and they become one flesh" (Genesis 2:24 NIV).

All this is true because God had an end in mind for marriage that goes beyond my happiness, my comfort, or my desire to be loved. God designed marriage to make us holy. God is in the saint-making business, and marriage is one of His best tools. Any relationship that calls me to confront my selfishness and spend my time learning how to love and serve another person, even when I know all their faults, is a powerful tool to make me look like Jesus and to illustrate His grace to the world.

Marriage Demands God's Grace

I find myself smiling at the disciples. They heard what Jesus said about marriage and there was a collective gulp. "If this is the situation between a husband and wife, it is better not to marry" (Matthew 19:10 NIV). Take the time to read how Jesus responds for yourself, but here is how I summarize it: Basically, Jesus said, "You've got that right. Marriage is tough and demanding, and some people shouldn't get married." (Matthew 19:11) That is why we used to have the line in traditional marriage vows, "It is not to be entered into lightly, but soberly, reverently, and in the fear of God."

Why so somber and foreboding? Because this process of "becoming one" is demanding and undertaken in purely human strength, or with purely human intention. It will lead to the problem the Pharisees were experiencing: "hardness of heart." Every marriage begins because some passion of heart brought a man and woman together. What happens between "this is the person for me" and "I don't love this person anymore"? Life happens. Sin happens. We get distracted. We start getting selfish. "She doesn't do this," and "he doesn't do that," then poof—one day you wake up and things aren't what they once were. The passion that leads to the perseverance required to become "soul mates" is not found in the human heart. It is found in God's grace and strength.

So let me end this chapter like a pastor. If we want something that we once had, we must do something that we once did. Jesus said it this way: "Repent and do the things you did at first" (Revelation 2:5 NIV). Jesus mentioned one typical reason for the implosion of marriages, which is adultery (Matthew 19:9). But as we said early on, it isn't the big things like that—it is the little things we have stopped doing or have given up on.

Maybe it is time to turn to God and ask for grace rather than permission. Maybe the prayer should be, "Lord, can You help us make this marriage all it can be?" rather than, "Lord, can You give me a way out of this marriage?" Ask Him to remind you of the things that brought you together. Ask Him to renew your commitment to honor Him in obedience. Pray to Him for the grace it takes to experience the joy of making a soul mate and "becoming one."

Chapter 6 Notes

_____

_____

_____

_____

_____

_____

_____

_____

_____

_____

_____

_____

_____

_____

_____

_____

_____

_____

_____

_____

_____

_____

CHAPTER SEVEN

I Knew You Would Mess Up

"Simon, Simon, Satan has asked to sift all of you as wheat. But I have prayed for you, Simon, that your faith may not fail. And when you have turned back, strengthen your brothers."

But he replied, "Lord, I am ready to go with you to prison and to death."

Jesus answered, "I tell you, Peter, before the rooster crows today, you will deny three times that you know me." — **Luke 22:31-34 (NIV)**

Sane people do not consider traveling from Florida to Indiana in November. The migration typically runs in the other direction. But we have family in Indiana and the holidays were upon us, so we drove up to spend a week. Mid-visit, we met my sisters for lunch at Panera Bread, or as my father calls it, the "Dry-Bread Restaurant."

We ate and laughed with them until they had to return to work. After the goodbyes, my wife and I lingered at the table, finishing our meal, when our five-year-old little girl broke off the conversation she was having with her stuffed animal "Kitty" and asked, "Mom what does it mean when you give somebody the middle finger?"

Jenelle looked at me bug-eyed, which caused Emily Rose to look at me bug-eyed, which caused me to stuff a hunk of dry bread in my mouth. So with great parenting wisdom, my wife asked, "Why do you want to know that, Emily Rose?"

"Because Michael, in our class, gave another boy the middle finger and my friend Gionna says when you do that it is really bad because it means the F word."

"Well, Emily Rose, what is the F word?" Jenelle asked, causing me to choke on the dry bread stuffed in my mouth.

Emily whispered, "Mommy, I can't say it. It's the nastiest word."

Jenelle smiled and reassured her, "It's all right honey, just say it in my ear."

Emily cupped her hands around Jenelle's ear and whispered the vile word.

"Oh," said Jenelle, "Well, honey, why don't you tell your daddy what the F word is." I looked at her bug-eyed and braced myself as my little girl whispered the world's nastiest word to me:

"Failure."

The Real "F Word"

Failure may be our real "F word." We demand perfection of ourselves even though the evidence overwhelmingly proves that we are really pros at failure.

We see failure as an unmentionable possibility. Jesus knows it is an inevitable reality. We are all going to fail. We are going to mess up often and sometimes in huge ways. At times, our failures are going to hurt others whom we care about.

When Christ warns the disciples of impending failure, Peter thrusts out his chest and declares, "Lord, I got Your back. No matter what, I will never leave You, I will never let You down, I will never deny You, even if I have to die with You."

Peter meant every word! He knew that he loved Jesus. Maybe you feel exactly the same way. I do not doubt your sincerity. We all have commitments we think are absolutes and behaviors we think are inconceivable. Peter knew he was a lot of things, but a coward wasn't one of them. There was no way that he was going to abandon his rabbi and friend when Jesus needed him most. Yet that is exactly what he did. So while we are repulsed by the idea of failure, we may need to think differently about the subject. This is especially true if you are currently living in the backwash of your own failure.

A Battle That Is Too Big for Us

Jesus told Peter that Satan had asked to sift him. Well, that's big news and should have intimidated Peter a little, or at least given him pause. However, Peter was bold and blustery: "I am ready—bring him on!" One of the greatest mistakes that we make is thinking that we can withstand temptation in our own strength. On your best day, you are not good enough to be holy. At the apex of our natural virtue, we cannot sustain our walk of faith.

The Christian life is often described as warfare. Church fathers and reformers told us that we face three terrible enemies: the world, the flesh, and the devil. Each of them is formidable. Each of them is too powerful for us with only our own strength. We are told that we put to death the works of our flesh "through the Spirit," and Paul admonishes us to "be strong in the Lord and in his mighty power. Put on the full armor of God, so that you can take your stand against the devil's schemes" (Ephesians 6:10-11 NIV).

This "putting on the whole armor of God" sounds like mere rhetorical flourish on Paul's part, but it is more practical than we realize. None of us knows exactly how it works, but I do know that it involves intentional behaviors on my part. One of the first things I do each morning, after coffee of course, is think about what I will put on for the day. What attire does the weather and my responsibilities for the day demand? "Putting on the whole armor of God" means that we wake up every day and realize that we are going to face challenges and temptations that demand God's resources and not ours. So we take the time to read, pray, meditate, and prepare our hearts to be strong in the Lord and in the power of His might. Without this whole armor, we are not equipped to handle the daily battles.

The Lord Has a Purpose, Even for Our Failures

Did you notice that Jesus said to Peter, "Satan has asked to sift all of you as wheat" (NIV)?

Though every nuance of meaning in this scripture may not be clear, the verse does communicate the truth that Christ, not Satan, is in charge. Satan had to get Christ's permission to touch Peter, and any of us. This means that nothing comes into my life that doesn't first pass through the hands of my God. Yes, we face a formidable enemy, but he bows to our almighty Savior. And if our Lord allows us to experience temptations, heartaches, and even failure in our lives, there is a redemptive purpose in it.

Satan was given permission to "sift" us, but not to destroy us. Sifting is a process in which flour, or other substances, are winnowed or passed through a sieve in order to remove coarse and useless pieces so that only what is good and useful remains. The Scriptures tell us that God "causes all things to work together for the good of those who love God, to those who are called according to His purpose" (Romans 8:28 NIV).

That verse does not say that God "causes all things"; it says He "causes all things to work together for good." There is a divine alchemy by which the Lord takes even things that were intended for evil, failures we were permitted to experience, and redeems them for His purpose to conform us to the image of His Son.

Cooperating with the Process

Sifting is not endured by heroism but by honesty. And honesty is much more difficult than heroism. When the Lord allows our faith to be sifted, He is going to bring junk to the surface of our hearts. Heroism faces the demons without, but honesty has to confess the demons within. It forces us to confess that we really are weak and selfish, and given the right circumstances, any of us are capable of the worst forms of betrayal and most cowardly acts of self-preservation.

Failure is a terrible experience, but it is a powerful sieve. It sifts the pride and self-sufficiency. It sifts the judgment and legalism. It leaves behind grace, kindness, understanding, humility, and forgiveness. The person who has never experienced failure, or more correctly, has not owned up to it, is usually an intolerable drag on everyone else's heart. People cannot respect them because of their insincerity and hypocrisy. The Scriptures tell us that when we enter the church, we are entering a company of people who are "being made perfect." Believe it or not, failure is one step in the process of our perfection.

In Luke 22:32, Jesus was telling Peter that God can and does redeem our pain and failures:

And when you have turned, strengthen your brothers.
(NIV)

In other words, no hurt is wasted in God's economy.

A few years ago, my wife and I bought a Ford Windstar minivan. Up until that time, I had never heard of a Windstar. I didn't know they existed, even though I had probably driven by a dozen a week. Once I owned one, I began to see them everywhere. I even began to feel a kinship with other people who had the smarts to buy the same minivan that I did. After I owned my Windstar for a few years and learned that I had made a huge mistake in ever buying the rolling piece of junk, I felt a different sort of kinship with Windstar owners. If someone ever says to me, "I bought a Windstar," I do not need to hear anything else. I sympathize immediately. I know how to comfort them and pray for them. I have made the same mistake. I have lived with the regrets of that decision.

I do hope you are smiling, but here is my thought: This is how God redeems all of our experiences of pain and failure. When we have endured our own failures, humiliation, and sin, isn't it amazing how we can spot others who are struggling just as we have? Isn't it part of God's grace that He equips us to comfort others with the same comfort we received from Him?

No pain is wasted; no failure goes unredeemed. Our God is so awesome that if we keep faith, He can redeem even our failures for others' good and His glory.

Jesus Doesn't Quit on Us When We Fail

"But I have prayed for you…"
That means our failures are not fatal!
"I have prayed for you, Simon, that your faith may not fail" (Luke 22:32 NIV). Simon was about to fail *big*

time! But Jesus makes a distinction between our personal failures and failure of our faith. Failure is not the end of our faith and it's not the end of our relationship to our God. The key is what we will do when we fail.

It is in the crucible of failure that the deceiver does some of his greatest work. When we fail miserably, when we are left in the dark weeping bitterly over broken promises and shattered aspirations, what will we do? Where will we turn? The temptation will be to despair about our efforts to be what God tells us we can be. Or there will be a temptation to bitterness and anger. We will be tempted to shake our fist at God for allowing us to go through such pain and humiliation. It is not the failure that would sever our connection to God, it is whether we will still have faith then.

I have sat in gloomy circles with married couples after the discovery that one is cheating on the other. Outside of death, it is difficult for me to imagine a situation that is more painful. The difference is that the one who caused the pain is still very much alive. The source of this excruciating heartache lives with us. The hardest words to utter in that moment are even far more difficult to believe: "If you want to, you can still make it work. God can heal your heart, and He can pour new love for one another in there."

Then I pause, as if that wasn't difficult enough for them to believe, and I whisper, "And God can still use you. Even this failure, ugly and painful as it is, can be redeemed for His purposes. The Lord can pull you out of this dark hole and use both of you to turn and strengthen others."

Every time I say that, I know they don't believe me. The ones who are trying to be kind will give a silent, tearful nod. Others have sneered at my "church talk" attempt at reassurance. However, I have witnessed God's divine alchemy too often to let human cynicism deter me. I know God can do it. In fact, I have seen the Lord use what we would consider our greatest failures to propel us into the years of our deepest and most effective ministry. Personal pain and failures change the focus of the ministry we do, from building better ministries to wanting to "strengthen the brethren."

Faith is so often viewed as something we need to move great mountains in the world around us. But the greatest act of faith you may ever have to show is to turn back to a loving God and believe He can still use you, that He still loves you, and that He still wants to bless you even after you have failed in the worst way. We don't lose because we fail—God knew we were going to fail. The only way we lose is if we lose faith.

Chapter 7 Notes

CHAPTER EIGHT

Jesus Doesn't Work for Most People

They said to him, "John's disciples often fast and pray, and so do the disciples of the Pharisees, but yours go on eating and drinking."

Jesus answered, "Can you make the guests of the Bridegroom fast while he is with them? But the time will come when the Bridegroom will be taken away from them; in those days they will fast."

He told them this parable: "No one tears a piece out of a new garment to patch an old one. Otherwise, they will have torn the new garment, and the patch from the new will not match the old. And no one pours new wine into old wineskins. Otherwise, the new wine will burst the skins; the wine will run out and the wineskins will be ruined. No, new wine must be poured into new wineskins. And no one after drinking old wine wants the new, for they say, 'The old is better.'" — **Luke 5:33-39 (NIV)**

We had just finished a big Sunday at church. Every seat had been filled and the ushers had to bring in more. By the time people finished walking in, there were seats all the way from the front stage to the rear tech booth, with a crowd standing along the walls. The crowd brought great excitement and energy to the worship service.

I stood in the foyer afterward shaking hands and sharing pleasantries with people who were exiting. The entire time, one of our elders was hovering nearby waiting for a chance to speak with me. When a break in the stream of guests appeared, he slid up beside me and said, "Pastor Jack, what a day! We are seeing a lot of new faces in our church and that's great."

He paused, edged closer, and lowered his voice. I am supposing to avoid being picked up on the wiretap. He whispered, "But we lose so many of them. The majority come, they hang around for a few weeks or months, and then they disappear."

I nodded my head. He was looking for more. When he saw that a brilliant solution or profound explanation wasn't forthcoming, he was more direct.

"What can we do to stop that? What can we do to get them to stick around and commit?"

Now, I usually try to be a diplomatic leader. I try to make sure I understand the concern behind questions and respond in a way that invites more discussion and input. I am a great guy that way. But it was right after church on Sunday and I was tired. So in a moment of unguarded honesty, I answered, "Not much."

I may not have said it right, but what I said was right. In nearly three decades of pastoral ministry, I have dealt with many people and wrestled with many concerns over their spiritual condition. I have witnessed hundreds of people, maybe thousands, enthusiastically begin some sort of "spiritual" pursuit of God and Christ. I have also seen many of them lose that enthusiasm and drift away.

I have sat in meeting after meeting with other church leaders. We have struggled to find ways to "make church more relevant to contemporary needs and concerns" and "close the back door" so that people will stay, connect, commit, and begin to mature in their relationship with Christ. I have read books, bought systems, and attended conferences for years. I have read blogs that can explain to us the "real" reason why men, women, seniors, busters, boomers, and millennials are leaving our churches. I have now arrived at a point where, considering all the explanations that have been given for the falling away of some and the lack of interest in others, I think they are all wrong.

When I study the array of programs and strategies that are recommended to church leaders, on the basis that they will provide compelling reasons for the latest disenchanted group to reconsider the church and reengage in the faith, I have decided they are mostly a waste of time. Especially for that special breed of spiritual soul that has grown more prevalent and popular in our world. Such a person, whether Christian or non-Christian, declares, "I don't have a problem with Jesus, but I have real problems with the church."

Despite their protests and the many splendidly self-serving and sanctimonious arguments that they post on Facebook, Twitter, or share profoundly while sipping an overpriced latte at Starbucks, I must say that they are blowing smoke. Okay, maybe they are sincerely mistaken. Either way, they are wrong.

Their problem really is with Jesus. The church could adapt the most cutting-edge and creative forms of presenting a message, become a radical champion for whatever the latest hot-button social issue of the day happens to be, or offer a buffet line of support groups and counseling opportunities that touch the "felt needs" of our culture. Yet we will still find that the genuine faith Jesus came to make available is the problem. It doesn't fit with our plans. Jesus just "doesn't work" for many people.

This fact, and people being blind to it, is not a new situation. The parable that Jesus shared in Luke 5 was a response to the Pharisees. They would not affiliate with Jesus, and they were trying to give a reason why. Jesus and his disciples did not "fast often," as the Pharisees did, or even like the disciples of John the Baptist. So the Pharisees said, "We don't follow you because you don't take fasting and personal denial as seriously as we think you should." Don't get hung up on the fasting issue. Today people will say they refuse to align with Jesus and His followers because we don't take social justice seriously enough, or we don't place enough attention on experiential and communal worship, or because we don't emphasize introspection to the level that other religions or even other churches do.

Jesus's response in this brief exchange highlights the real reasons why He, and the faith He came to make available, will just never do the trick for some people. It is a fascinating interaction.

Jesus Refuses to Pander

When the Pharisees expressed concern to Jesus about a lack of proper attentiveness to their religious practices, you can almost hear all the unspoken words squeezed between what is actually verbalized:

"Jesus, we have been watching you and your followers. We like some of what we see. However, there is the issue of fasting. Fasting is an important practice and highly valued in this community, and your followers show insensitivity toward it. You might have a larger following and broader acceptance if you would just make that minor adjustment."

Jesus answer is basically: "The people who follow Me respond to Me, not the other way around."

In other words, Christians do not fast to fit in, look respectable, or gain the approval of the culture around them. Believers fast because of the relationship they have with Jesus. If they sense Him near and are celebrating His presence, then fasting is not necessary. If they feel the need to draw closer to Jesus, then they fast. However, they do not engage in spiritual disciplines, or neglect to do so, based upon how it affects those around them.

The world is full of people, political parties, and religious groups that try to emphasize or downplay aspects of Jesus's character for their own purposes. Jesus would be more palatable and less offensive if He didn't have such a narrow view of marriage. Jesus would relate better to the culture if He didn't insist upon rich people being held accountable for the poor, the widow, and the orphan. If Jesus would become the champion of animal's rights or the poster boy of their cause, He would be perfect. Everyone would love to be Jesus's political advisor, instructing Him on how to increase His approval ratings. But Jesus isn't looking for advisors—He is looking for followers. Followers of Christ do and refuse to do things for one motive: their response to the person of Jesus.

And Jesus is an equal opportunity offender—of religious and irreligious zealots, capitalists and communists, and liberals and conservatives. Jesus does not ask His church to adjust to suit the preferences of the culture; He demands that anyone who follows Him learn to live in response to Him and adjust to be a part of His family. We live and respond to life on His terms. Then there is another reason Jesus doesn't "work" for many people:

Jesus Refuses to Be a "Patch Job" for Our Life

*No one tears a piece out of a new garment to patch an old one. Otherwise, they will have torn the new garment, and the patch from the new will not match the old. — **Luke 5:36 (NIV)***

If you own a suit that has a rip in the seams and you do not want to spend the money to buy a new suit, you try to fix the problem cheaply by getting a tailor to mend the seam. If you get a flat tire and new tires are too expensive, you find someone to patch the old tire or plug the hole.

Jesus used the phrase "a new garment to patch an old one" because He knew that many people came to Him looking for a "patch job" on their lives. We are looking for Him to slap a piece of new cloth onto our old way of life. We don't want to change completely, but we have very specific holes we are looking to get patched up. This manner of approach to Jesus has never changed.

People get very interested in church or "religion" when they are struggling in their marriages and have the idea that Jesus could be the fix. Frustrated parents are willing to give church "a shot" as a way to mend a relationship with a rebellious child. Sick people will run to Jesus when they need Him to heal some part of their bodies, and people in debt will pray if it helps them get their finances fixed up.

It is not awful that these felt needs make us think of Jesus, but the problem is with our lack of long-term understanding. Yes, we want Him to patch up these damaged areas, but we don't want Him to mess with the parts of our lives that we are comfortable with and feel are doing fine. We are looking for a very specific and targeted patch job. This doesn't work for a variety of reasons, but here is one that may not be immediately apparent to us: often, it is the parts of our lives we are most comfortable with that are causing struggles in other areas and that most need to change.

We humans are systemic beings. Our survival and happiness is dependent upon a respiratory, circulatory, nervous, muscular, skeletal, and digestive system. These systems are all connected to and reliant upon one another. If there is a pain or dysfunction in my muscular system, it can be caused by a dysfunction in any of the other systems and will have an impact on all those systems.

The same is true of spiritual life. It is impossible to see health and healing in our lives if we approach the aspects of our lives as segregated and isolated from one another. Finances, romances, families, and emotions—all of these things are spiritual and are an interconnected whole in our lives. The Scriptures tell us that all the "issues" of our life flow from the condition of our hearts. So, if I am undisciplined in my finances and go into debt, if I don't budget well and overspend, then that behavior will lead to emotional stress, which in turn may lead to tension in my marriage and so forth.

So Jesus doesn't do patchwork. He won't fix your marriage but leave your money alone. He won't deal with your broken heart and leave your bitterness unaddressed. He wants to fix all of us. It's a whole new wardrobe or nothing.

You were taught, with regard to your former way of life, to put off your old self, which is being corrupted by its deceitful desires; to be made new in the attitude of your minds, and to put on the new self, created to be like God in true righteousness and holiness. — **Ephesians 4:22-24 (NIV)**

"...you have taken off your old self with its practices and have put on the new self, which is being renewed in

knowledge in the image of its Creator." — ***Colossians 3:9-10*** **(NIV)**

Everything changes when we come to Christ, not just the parts of our lives where we see the rips, holes, and malfunctions. That doesn't work for people who only want help financially, but do not want accountability relationally. It isn't palatable for people who want Jesus to heal their bodies, but do not want him to mess with the eating habits or alcoholism with which they are comfortable. People who only want Jesus to make their marriage run more smoothly, but don't want him to deal with their anger or selfishness, begin to lose interest. They are looking for patchwork on lives they are comfortable with, not transformation to a life that honors God. This brings us to the biggest reason Jesus doesn't "work" for many people

We Simply Don't Understand the Nature of the Gospel

And no one pours new wine into old wineskins. Otherwise, the wine will burst the skins, and both the wine and the wineskins will be ruined. No, they pour new wine into new wineskins. — ***Mark 2:22 (NIV)***

The gospel enters a life, if it enters at all, as new wine. It is alive, bubbling, fermenting, expanding, and stretching. It is "Christ in you." That is the nature of the gospel. You cannot enter into a relationship with Jesus and stay the same. The Spirit of God is going to come in, full of expansive and transforming life. He is going to challenge every category of truth and behavior with which you have grown comfortable. Your views about morality, about ethics, about other people, about generosity—yes, even about politics—will be stretched.

If we have not been made new and malleable through repentance and genuine faith, we will not be able to deal with the power of the true gospel. It will not be held comfortably in the wineskins of our old paradigms, lifestyles, and values.

Therein lies the struggle. When it comes to those things, we are all in the powerful grip of the status quo. Jesus says, "When you have gotten used to old wine, you will not want the new." We grow comfortable with our old life and our old self. We like the taste and feel of our old, selfish, and sinful ways. We like the comfort of being able to justify our actions and opinions. We enjoy the benefits we receive from the system at work or the political system in our community, even if that system is unfair and corrupt. The gospel will not just deal with what we are uncomfortable with and makes us unhappy; it will challenge the parts with which we are comfortable and happy but still need to change.

The new wine of the gospel will expand our sense of responsibility for others. It will open our eyes to see things like fairness and justice bigger than we ever have before. That may be very good for us, but it also is very uncomfortable. We do not want to change, we do not want to be challenged, we do not want God to come pouring into our lives with all this truth. We don't want the chaos of having our beliefs and our behavioral patterns all messed up. We don't want the discomfort of having our circle of understanding and compassion expanded by the new life of Christ in us.

So we keep trying to get by spiritually "on the cheap." We keep looking for solutions that are convenient and bring us peace with a minimal amount of fuss and bother.

Jesus doesn't work for us because He comes to our hearts with His own agenda and life, and we are required to give ours up to receive His. We may not want that, but we need it so desperately. And Jesus cares too deeply to offer us the religious placebos that are popular in our world. When we can truly learn to follow Jesus, we will see that we work for Jesus.

Chapter 8 Notes

CHAPTER NINE

"You! Yes, You. Come, Follow Me!"

As Jesus went on from there, he saw a man named Matthew sitting at the tax collector's booth. "Follow me," he told him, and Matthew got up and followed him.

While Jesus was having dinner at Matthew's house, many tax collectors and sinners came and ate with him and his disciples. When the Pharisees saw this, they asked his disciples, "Why does your teacher eat with tax collectors and sinners?"

*On hearing this, Jesus said, "It is not the healthy who need a doctor, but the sick. But go and learn what this means: 'I desire mercy, not sacrifice.' For I have not come to call the righteous, but sinners." — **Matthew 9:9-13 (NIV)***

The more complex a subject is, the more we are dependent upon revelation to understand it. If I want to learn about a rock, the rock doesn't have to reveal anything to me. I can learn all I need to about a rock on my own. However, learning about a dog will take longer and require me to relate to the dog in some fashion. Still, dogs are fairly straightforward creatures and I can learn all I need to know simply by interaction and observation. When it comes to learning about another human being, however, there are certain things I can never know about them if they do not reveal themselves to me. I cannot know what makes them happy or sad, what inspires them, or what they believe or dream unless they reveal themselves to me. They have to give me a word.

Now let's think about God. There are some things we can learn about God by observing His creation, but we will never know the most important things about God unless He reveals himself to us. God has to give us the Word—and that is exactly what the Lord did for us in Jesus.

If I were to ask ten people to tell me what the word *faith* means, I think I would get eleven definitions. That is why I am so grateful that God sent Jesus. One of the primary reasons Jesus came was to explain, or to reveal, God to us. "The Word became flesh and made his dwelling among us. We have seen his glory, the glory of the one and only Son, who came from the Father, full of grace and truth" (John 1:14 NIV). Jesus was God's revelation of Himself to us.

We needed that revelation desperately. A few verses later, John wrote, "For the law was given through Moses, grace and truth came through Jesus Christ" (John 1:17 NIV). Jesus came not only to reveal the nature of God to us, but also to make it clear how we can relate to Him. Until He arrived, the only route to that relationship was the law. There were two problems with that approach. First, we couldn't keep the law. Second, people had corrupted the law. Over thousands of years, they had taken that law and complicated and stratified it to such an extent that being in a relationship with God left us lost in a maze of rules and regulations. So when Jesus arrived, He made a relationship with God simple again.

Before we get too happy, let me be clear about one thing: Just because something is simple doesn't mean it's easy. A few years ago a friend talked me into taking up the game of golf. Golf is a simple game. The object is to get the ball in the hole. That is simple, but it is hardly easy. Golf is one of the most aggravating, challenging, exasperating, demanding, and enjoyable games I have ever played. No matter how long you play, you can still improve. Living by faith is the same way. It is simple, but it is very demanding—and rewarding.

Faith Begins with a Response to an Invitation

I have always had misgivings about the way these stories are told in the Scriptures. Take Matthew, for example: he had a business, and he was doing well. Jesus came up to him, right in the middle of the business day, and said, "Drop everything and follow me," and Matthew did it! He got up right then and left everything to follow Jesus. I have wondered at times whether the Gospels record it that way to clean it up a bit. Or whether the story kind of morphed into this version years later. I have witnessed how "salvation stories" in church tend to go through that process. "Why, I remember the night I was saved at camp meeting. On the eighty-second verse of 'Just As I Am,' I put down my whiskey bottle, jumped over six pews, and landed on my knees in front of the altar, got up sober, and preached the sermon!"

The problem is this wasn't just Matthew's story; this happened to many of the first followers of Jesus. When you read the stories of Peter, Andrew, James, and John, you see the same pattern: Jesus approached them and issued a simple but immediate and dramatic invitation, "Come, follow Me." Amazingly, they dropped everything to do just that. Still, it begs the question: "Why would they do that? Why did Matthew respond so quickly?"

He Recognized an Incredible Opportunity

Many scholars and teachers have written extensively over the last several years to remind us that Jesus was a rabbi. Jesus was referred to, or referred to Himself, as a rabbi fifty-four times in the New Testament. If you were a Jewish boy in the first century, the greatest achievement you could have would be to become a rabbi. In order for that to happen, you had to be a disciple or mentored by a man who was already recognized as a rabbi. So young men who had this aspiration would often approach them and ask, "Can I follow you?" Jesus had that happen to Him: "As they were walking along the road, a man said to him, 'I will follow you wherever you go'" (Luke 9:52). Most often the answer from a typical rabbi was no. Only the best and brightest were accepted into the entourage of a reputable rabbi. It was a once-in-a-lifetime opportunity.

But Matthew did not seek out Jesus—he was invited by Jesus. He recognized the opportunity.

He Knew Something About Himself

Only the best of the best get into rabbinical school. But Matthew was collecting taxes. That means he didn't make the cut. Matthew wasn't good enough. He was washed out and washed up when it came to being a rabbi. He had given up on the dream a long time ago. So had all the other disciples of Jesus, but for Matthew it was worse. Not only had he given up on trying to be good enough to be a rabbi, but Matthew had also given up on being good at all and had turned to collecting taxes.

I had to take some time to explain to you how great it was to become a rabbi, but most of you know instinctively how bad it is to become a tax collector. As bad as it may seem now, it was heinous then. Israel was an occupied country. Their captors, the Romans, levied the taxes on them and they would sell rights, or "tax booth franchises," to locals in order to collect the taxes. The Romans had no love for the Jewish people, so they didn't care what was charged over the actual tax as long as they got theirs, and they supplied the muscle to make sure everyone paid up. Most tax collectors took advantage of that reality to skim a lucrative income off of their neighbors and kin.

If you were a tax collector for Rome, then you were a traitor for sure and a cheat most likely. When Jewish people wrote or spoke about tax collectors, the word usually appeared in the phrase "tax collectors and sinners" (Matthew 9:10 NIV). Tax collectors got their own category of disdain. There were "sinners" and then there were "tax collectors." You have your murderers, rapists, prostitutes, all those kinds, on one hand; but then, in a category all to themselves, you have *tax collectors*. They had sold out their faith, their family, their country, and their culture. They were the worst!

Matthew knew people felt that way about him, and frankly, he probably felt that way about himself. Many of us can look back at a point in life where we made decisions and took actions that were counter to all our values—where we sold out our principles in the face of temptation or pressure. Where we caved in and compromised in order to keep a client, or a boyfriend, or a job, or a reputation. We know we were sinners and sellouts, that we have cheated and violated, knowing and that all of the good, religious folks would hate us if they knew or do hate us because they do know. So not only was Matthew not good enough to be a rabbi, he wasn't even allowed to go to the temple anymore because he was considered unclean.

Imagine you're Matthew. You aren't sending out applications to rabbinical school anymore, are you? Shoot, you are so far gone that you don't even bother to go to church anymore. Then one day a rabbi comes to your booth—and not just any rabbi, but Jesus, the rabbi whose teaching prompts people to say, "Never man spake like this man" (John 7:46 KJV). A rabbi with healing in His wings! He walks up to your tax booth and says, "I want you to follow Me. I want you to enter My school. I want you to be My disciple."

John Ortberg pastors a Presbyterian Church in Menlo Park, California. A vice president of the San Francisco Giants attends the church, and he shared a story with Ortberg about a scouting trip he took to see a young pitcher in the Dominican Republic. After he had spent an afternoon watching some of the players work out, the VP told Ortberg that a sixteen-year-old kid walked up to him with tears in his eyes and shook his hand.

Ortberg writes:

> All right, now, imagine, you're a sixteen-year-old kid in the Dominican Republic. You've got no father. You've got no money. You've got no education. You've got no prospects. You're destined to live a life in poverty that will be pretty brief and then die. And then one day, the vice president of the San Francisco Giants comes along and looks you in the eye, and says to you, I think you've got what it takes, come and follow me. Now would you go follow him, or would you say, "No thanks, I think I'll just stay here in the Dominican Republic"? You would drop everything. You would run, with tears in your eyes.[12]

So here was Matthew—he wasn't smart enough, he wasn't spiritual enough, and he had completely blown it with his life. But Jesus said to him, "I believe in you. I believe you have what it takes. Come and follow Me." No wonder he dropped everything to do it! That is the way faith begins. Because let me tell you something else: Rabbis never went out and recruited followers. To do that was beneath their dignity. People ran to them. People tried to prove to them that they were good enough.

Religion still behaves that way. Churches are still full of people running around trying to prove that they are good enough and to earn the approval and acceptance of God. But the Christian faith starts with God coming after us. Jesus says to us all, "You did not choose me, but I chose you..." (John 15:16 NIV). We didn't go looking for God—He came looking for us, and more amazingly, He called us to follow Him.

> *Brothers and sisters, think of what you were when you were called...God chose the foolish things of the world...God chose the weak things of the world...God chose the lowly things and the despised things—and the things that are not—to nullify the things that are...* — *1 Corinthians 1:26-28 (NIV)*

Faith begins in that moment when the Living Lord walks into your life and sees all the failures, but still invites you to follow Him and become His disciple.

What Does the Choice Mean?

Now you have a choice to make. Will you drop everything in your life? The call to follow Jesus may mean you leave your job or leave your home. Then again, maybe He will call you to serve Him right where you are. Regardless, when Jesus comes and says, "I want you to be My disciple," He means, "From this moment on, the number one goal in your life is to be with Me every moment, to learn from Me how to become like Me, and to live under the care and love of this God who loves you more than you could possibly imagine."

Maybe you think you don't have enough faith. But you know what? Jesus believes in you. That's what the story of the call of the disciples is about. The amazing thing is not that they would believe in Jesus; it's that He believed in them. And He believes in you and me.

The Beginning of a Lifelong Relationship

Gordon MacDonald wrote of a conversation he had with a friend who was skeptical about Christians and Christianity.[13] As they were eating breakfast, his friend asked, "what is this 'thing' about 'accepting Christ'? I can't relate to that language at all."

"We are talking about a relationship that is personal and dynamic and life-altering," MacDonald responded.

"Well, that's another matter," his friend said. "But I don't understand how that could begin by accepting Christ. I can't think of any relationship that goes very far by just accepting a person. I mean, I accept you. All that means is I am willing to let you be you and not make a big deal out of it. But then what? Where do things go from there? So 'accepting Jesus' doesn't make much sense to me."

MacDonald sipped his coffee and offered, "then, how about 'following Christ'? That means living with Him and learning to look at life and live it as He did."

"So you are saying that accepting Christ and following Christ are the same thing. Why don't you call yourselves 'Christ-followers' then? I can understand that better than 'accepting Jesus,'" the friend asked.

MacDonald said that ever since that conversation, he has called himself a Christ-follower. I think he is on to something. Jesus did not ask us to 'accept Him'; He said, "Follow me." Faith involves entering into a full-time relationship with Jesus that affects, influences, and changes our entire lives. That becomes apparent when Matthew responds to Jesus's invitation to follow Him and they immediately go to Matthew's house. Faith takes Jesus home with it!

The faith that pleases our God is a faith that enters our lives. Religion goes to church to meet Jesus. It spends an hour a week with Him, leaves a few dollars for His business, and says *amen* while thinking, "Okay Jesus, I will think about what we talked over today, see You next week...or next month...or next Easter." Faith puts you in a relationship, and that means Jesus goes home with you. And when you get home, He tells you what to do. Faith simply impacts every area of your life. It is a complete and consuming relationship.

We Learn by Imitating

Jesus once issued this invitation: "Take my yoke upon you and learn from me..." (Matthew 11:29 NIV). A rabbi's teaching was sometimes called his "yoke." It is a great word picture. If you had a young ox and you wanted to train it to plow, you hitched it up in a yoke with an older, more experienced ox. Oxen learned by pulling together. That is the way we learn from Jesus.

We learn by pulling through life with Him. We learn by listening to Him, feeling His impulse, and responding to His pull as we navigate marriage, parenting, and the rest of our lives. We learn by doing life with Him. We do not learn by attending church, memorizing catechisms, and listening to sermons. We get down on our knees and ask, "Master, how should I respond? What attitude should I have? How much should I give? What should I say? Do You see something I am not seeing?" And we learn to move at the impulse of His Spirit. We need to do that because transformation is the goal of faith. We are transformed by imitating the greatest teacher—Jesus.

> *...everyone who is fully trained will be like their teacher.*
> *— Luke 6:40 (NIV)*

People Who Follow Jesus Usually Have Profound Influence

One of the first things that Matthew did once he became a Christ-follower was to try to introduce his friends to Jesus. He threw a party. And guess who showed up? Other tax collectors and sinners, of course!

If Jesus has invited you to join Him, He hasn't invited you to isolate in a commune. He takes you right back to your house, to your neighborhood, and expects you to have influence over people who used to have influence over you. Jesus did this very quickly with Matthew. He had just become a Christ-follower and Jesus immediately said, "Let's throw a party and invite all your crazy sinner friends over." He didn't say, "Let me take you through a sixteen-week-long study on the book of Romans so you can correctly explain the doctrine of soteriology from a Pauline perspective." Thank God Jesus didn't do that. If Jesus calls you, He expects you to turn around and begin trying to influence your friends.

You are qualified. If you can barbecue and act like a Christian, you can be a witness. Jesus had to do this early in the process; He had Matthew throw a party quick, while people still want to go to his parties. They remembered the last party Matthew threw (well, at least they remembered the first part of the party Matthew threw, which was fun). This crowd wasn't going to show up at a Sunday school party.

What was Jesus thinking in all of this? He taught His followers that faith changes the way we see people: "It is not the healthy who need a doctor, but the sick. But go and learn what this means: 'I desire mercy, not sacrifice.' For I have not come to call the righteous, but sinners" (Matthew 9:12-13 NIV).

Jesus doesn't excuse sinners. Rather, He says they're sick, He says they are messed up, and He says that they need a physician. Most sinners know that already. They know their lives are a mess and they need a physician, a doctor, and a savior. Sin is a sickness that is too big for any of us, but the only person Jesus can't help is the person who doesn't think they need help.

He came to call sinners to repentance. Repentance means to hear the call of God and to change direction. It requires a decision to stop living how you choose and start following Him. He is calling you—yes you—to follow Him. If you hear that call and you want to make that choice, then do it. That is how it all begins.

Chapter 9 Notes

CHAPTER TEN

Money Isn't Your Problem

Someone in the crowd said to him, "Teacher, tell my brother to divide the inheritance with me."

Jesus replied, "Man, who appointed me a judge or an arbiter between you?" Then he said to them, "Watch out! Be on your guard against all kinds of greed; life does not consist in an abundance of possessions."

And he told them this parable: "The ground of a certain rich man yielded an abundant harvest. He thought to himself, 'What shall I do? I have no place to store my crops.'

"Then he said, 'This is what I'll do. I will tear down my barns and build bigger ones, and there I will store my surplus grain. And I'll say to myself, "You have plenty of grain laid up for many years. Take life easy; eat, drink and be merry."'

"But God said to him, 'You fool! This very night your life will be demanded from you. Then who will get what you have prepared for yourself?'

*"This is how it will be with whoever stores up things for themselves but is not rich toward God." — **Luke 12:13-21 (NIV)***

Fred Craddock once expressed a frustration to which all preachers and teachers can relate: "We wrestle with deep, spiritual truth and then after service, people shake our hands and ask us about ball games." This struggle to get present-minded people to consider eternal issues has always existed. Jesus dealt with it. Luke recounted an episode in which Jesus was trying to share warnings and encouragement concerning eternity with an audience, until He was interrupted by a man bored with all this religious talk. This man had *real* problems. He had money problems.

As spiritual as we all want to be, we need to admit that all the talk about heaven and hell may be good stuff to hear Jesus talk about in church, but Jesus adjudicating inheritance issues between hostile brothers is must-see TV. Even if our motives aren't purely voyeuristic, there are other reasons our ears perk up at this question. There are few people who don't worry about money on some level. So Jesus's response is important to us. As usual, His response wasn't at all what we would have expected.

Man, who appointed me judge or an arbiter between you?
— *Luke 12:14 (NIV)*

We aren't given many details about this guy's situation, but there is enough for us to know that somebody was done wrong and Jesus should fix it. That is what Jesus is supposed to do. That is why we come to church and sit through all those long, boring sermons—

so that when our lives get messed up, Jesus will fix it. That is the religious deal. We have an entire Christian industry that has grown up around the idea that this is what Jesus does. He exists to help us grow our businesses, be better leaders, have better sex lives, and fight for truth, justice, and the American way. Especially if we go to church.

But Jesus gave this man no plans, principles, or steps. In fact, He didn't even offer any sympathy. He basically said "if all you want to do is solve a legal issue, get a lawyer! But let Me help you deal with the real issue that is causing the problem." That is the way Jesus would respond to all of us who want Him to fix circumstances, but not to deal with our hearts. Jesus is not a life coach, credit negotiator, or even a marriage counselor. Christ teaches and works in us to change our hearts, not to manage our exterior situations.

So, when it comes to money, Jesus's words can be very disappointing. Lawyers can help you get settlement money, business consultants can help you make money, and financial advisors can help you save money, but only Jesus can teach you how to "handle money." And, when it comes to money, either you handle it or it handles you. Jesus did a lot of teaching about money, but He said two things over and over again:

Be Very Careful

Jesus warned His followers: "Watch out! Be on your guard against all kinds of greed; life does not consist in an abundance of possessions" (Luke 12:15 NIV).

God never wastes an experience. No matter what we are going through, we can learn from it. But we struggle because we get aggravated and seldom get educated. This man just wanted Jesus to get him out of the situation, but Jesus wanted to teach him something about the situation. When we are cheated or taken advantage of, rather than saying "Jesus, straighten this up," we may want to ask, "Lord, what do I need to learn about me in this situation?"

Here the tension was over money, and Jesus got serious fast: "Watch out!" Why was He so worried? It becomes clear that there are two times in life when money is a problem for us—when we have it and when we don't.

It seems odd that Jesus issued His urgent warning to the person who had no money in this situation. He was the one who got the shaft from his brother. It seems odd because we tend to think that money is only a problem for people who are loaded. But it is a problem for all of us all the time.

Notice Jesus didn't warn us to be on our guard against money. I have never had to protect myself from money because money has never come looking for me. Money has never intruded into my life with any great degree. Even when I worked for it, prayed for it, and pursued it, money has pretty much left me alone. However, the warning isn't about money: it is about *greed*. To help us grasp the danger, Jesus began a story:

*The ground of a certain rich man yielded an abundant harvest. He thought to himself, "What shall I do? I have no place to store my crops." — **Luke 12:16-17 (NIV)***

There is much to admire about the man in this parable. He is good at business and willing to take risks. He is a successful entrepreneur who has built a business and reinvested capital into expansion, and it has paid off big for him. We need people like that. We all benefit from people like that. Jesus didn't say to be on your guard against success or prosperity. Rather, He said to be on your guard against greed.

C. S. Lewis wrote that the devil doesn't create. God is the creator, and because we are created in His image, we can use our imagination and ingenuity to create. The devil, however, does not create. All the devil does is take healthy creations and pervert them. Sex is a good creation of God, but the devil attaches lust to sex and twists it into adultery. In the same way, hard work and success are good things, but greed is the demon that attaches to money and ruins it. It is one of the most dangerous demons we face.

*No one can serve two masters. Either he will hate the one and love the other, or he will be devoted to the one and despise the other. You cannot serve God and money. — **Matthew 6:24 (NIV)***

When Matthew recorded those words of Jesus, the word "Money" was capitalized. That is not a typo. When Jesus said it, he was referring to a being. In fact, in the King James Version it reads "Mammon." That was the name of an idol that pagans worshipped because they believed it would bring them prosperity. So the warning is against a spirit that attaches to money and exerts influence over us, perverts our approach to life, and pulls us away from God.

The man in the crowd could not listen to Jesus because he was too worried about money. Worry about money that makes you unable to hear and respond to Jesus is one of the signs of *Greed*. The demon of Greed is the strongest competitor you face for your loyalty to God. It wars against and dilutes every Christ-like virtue God wants to develop in you.

The Vice That Destroys Virtue

I could write an entire book of specific warnings about greed, but let me focus on just one example.

There are nine "fruits" of the Holy Spirit listed in the New Testament (Galatians 5:22-23), but Paul says that there are three that "abide": faith, hope, and love (1 Corinthians 13:13 NKJV). Love of money, and worry over it, will war against every one of those virtues in our lives. If we are obsessed and worried about money, we can't trust God. So we stop giving, we start working too many hours, and we do things we know are spiritual compromises to make money. And so we stop growing in faith.

Hope is always spoken of in the context of the Christian promise of eternal life. When that wealthy businessman describes his plans for his wealth, he says, "I'll say to myself, 'You have plenty laid up for many years. Take life easy; eat, drink, and be merry.'" Jesus didn't pick those words out of thin air. That was a philosophy of life that was used on the streets all the time. It's seen in 1 Corinthians 15:32: "If the dead are not raised, let us eat and drink, for tomorrow we die" (NIV).

That was the way of life for people who never thought of heaven and had no hope for it. Our Lord teaches us that we should live for eternity. Live like you are investing in treasures that will meet you when you arrive there. Greed whispers to our hearts: "eat, drink, and be merry. This life is as good as it gets. YOLO (You Only Live Once)."

The virtue of love means seeking the good of others over my own interests. Greed says, "I have to provide for me and mine first; that is my greatest duty in fact, so I better make sure I have plenty saved and stored up." This is the most dangerous thing about greed. No one thinks they are greedy. That entire approach seems so logical, but it can lead to withholding gifts you know you need to give and sacrifices that you are called to make. Greed is the failure to love.

Greed Is Pervasive

Paul once told Christians in Corinth to avoid associating with professed believers who were immoral.

Then he added, "[N]ot at all meaning the people of this world who are immoral, or the greedy and swindlers, or idolaters. In that case you would have to leave this world" (1 Corinthians 5:9-10 NIV). You have to love his realism. We are living in a world that is saturated with greed, among other vices.

My wife and I were enjoying a week away at one of our favorite beach retreats in Florida. On our second night there, she received a text message from her cousin telling us that she and her husband were also staying at a beach in Florida. They work with the Salvation Army, and we had not seen them in years. As they exchanged text messages, we learned that they were staying on the same beach—only a few miles away, in fact.

We made arrangements to meet them the next morning for breakfast at a little café that we love. The reason I enjoy it is that they serve you omelets as big as your head, a fact I shared enthusiastically with our relatives as we were enjoying our first cup of coffee. The husband is from England. He smiled at my enthusiasm over the size of the omelet I would soon devour and said, "Americans seem to have a fixation with surfeit." I laughed along with him but made a mental note to find out what "surfeit" meant as soon as I could. Later I did learn that he meant Americans have an insatiable desire for more. My first reaction was to think, "stupid Englishman. That is why we kicked your butts in the war!" After further reflection, however, I knew he was right. In fact, that very evening I watched a commercial for a wireless company built around this tag line: "No one ever stomped their feet and demanded less!" We live in a culture that depends on us demanding more and feeds that attitude in us. It is everywhere.

Greed Is Deceptive

The guy asking Jesus the question never would have imagined that he was the one who needed to worry about greed. He didn't have anything. That is why Jesus says, "watch out for Greed of all kinds!" Greed takes many forms. If it were just about money, all we would need to do is check our bank balance. But as it is, we have to check our hearts. Jesus told this story to help us see the symptoms of greed.

One is selfishness. The businessman in the story "thinks to himself," "says to himself," and within two verses uses *I*, *me*, or *mine* six times. In all his planning for how to make the money and what to do with it, the only meeting he ever called was with the only person he ever considered: himself. He never acknowledged God. He never looked up and said, "Lord, thanks for Your blessing. How do You want me to use it? What would You like for me to do with it?" He never thought about others. He had reached retirement, and his plans were to take life easy, hit the beach and the golf course, and build that nice retirement home in the mountains. There were never any thoughts of others

That's why God said, "you fool!" God wasn't addressing his intelligence; this man was obviously very intelligent. He was the CEO of a profitable agricultural business. Foolishness has to do with your heart, not your head. God called him a fool because he lived his whole life and never thought about his responsibility to serve God and others with what he had.

Another symptom of greed is constant, nagging dissatisfaction—the inability to enjoy what you have. This man was already extremely prosperous. The fact is, he had more than he needed. Every barn he owned was crammed to the rafters with stored-up wealth and profit. So what was his life plan? If every time you walk into your nice, 3 bedroom/2 bath house you want a 4 bedroom/3 bath; or if every time you drive your perfectly good minivan that can seat seven you tell yourself that you need a Crossover that seats eight; if it can't be Bahia grass because your neighbor put down St. Auggie's; if queen-sized isn't roomy enough and it has to be the king-sized; if it has to be "Better Homes and Gardens" not "Sufficient Homes and Gardens"; then you are struggling with Greed.

These examples lead us to the next symptom of greed—because you are greedy if you covet what others have. When we think about the guy who actually brought the complaint about his brother to Jesus, we aren't even sure if he had a legitimate beef. Maybe his father had divided the inheritance and he just wanted more of his brother's cut. I bet he was eaten up with jealousy over it.

There is another symptom of greed: anxiety. One is probably struggling with greed if they worry about money too much. That business owner was planning for retirement and seemed to be driven by a fear that he didn't have enough for the standard of living he was used to. So he kept piling it up and piling it up. One of the main emotions that leads us into the grip of greed is anxiety.

As soon as Jesus finished telling His parable to this man and His audience, He added these words: "Therefore, I tell you, do not worry about your life, what you will eat; or about your body, what you will wear...For the pagan world runs after all such things and your Father knows that you need them" (Luke 12:22, 30 NIV). In other words, if you get to where you are worried about money, you will start living like a pagan.

So, when it comes to money, the first thing Jesus says is: "be very careful." Then he says...

Be Very Generous

*This is how it will be with whoever stores up things for themselves but is not rich toward God. — **Luke 12:21** (NIV)*

The only antidote to the infectious demon of greed that is alluded to in this story is becoming "rich toward God." Jesus often talked this way. In another place He said:

*Do not store up for yourselves treasures on earth, where moths and vermin destroy, and where thieves break in and steal. But store up for yourselves treasures in heaven, where moths and vermin do not destroy, and where thieves do not break in and steal. — **Matthew 6:19-20 (NIV)***

These are not dreamy words, and this is not a mysterious process. We can use our resources to amass great wealth that will not last, or we can amass treasures that last eternally. And the only thing that is eternal about this earth is people. The way we become rich toward God and lay up treasures in heaven is by investing in the temporal good and eternal salvation of other people. So to be rich toward God, we have to become generous with other people.

Generosity is the only antidote to greed. It is interesting the way Jesus says it: "rich toward God." He doesn't say "rich with God." *Toward* is a directional word. I am either moving toward or away from something. This may seem an odd way for Him to say it, but there was a reason: wherever your money goes, your heart follows.

Early in my married life, I decided to try to prepare us for retirement through buying stocks. I researched and prepared for weeks before I actually bought my first shares of stock in a new start-up called Netflix. After I had made that investment in Netflix, what was initially an interest became an obsession. I read the financial section of the newspaper every day to see how the stock prices had done. I listened to financial radio programs to hear any news about the company that might affect the company value and stock price. Because Netflix had my money, it had my heart. Later in this very chapter, Jesus tells us, "Sell your possessions and give to the poor. Provide purses for yourselves that will not wear out, a treasure in heaven that will never fail…Where your treasure is, there your heart will be also" (Luke 12:33-34

NIV). When you decide that you are going to be radically generous to honor God and bless others, your heart will begin to move toward God; your heart will follow your treasure.

Last summer, my oldest son had the opportunity to step away from pursuing a degree in psychology and spend six months living and serving at a home for girls in the nation of Honduras. This home was started by members of our church to rescue and minister to young ladies whom had been sold into various forms of sex trafficking. As of this writing, twenty-six girls with twenty-six heart-breaking yet Christ-glorifying stories live there. My wife and I were worried about Zachary putting his education on hold for such a long time. We had wondered how soon he would get a job, start making some money, move out of our bedroom, etc. All the important and eternal things of the Kingdom. However, we agreed and it all fell into place.

I think the experience in Honduras had a more positive impact on our son than it did on the people he went to help. That always seems to be the case. I have never regretted the choice. However, I have never really understood how much I should value it until he wrote a blog post about his trip a few months after returning home. He wrote about his struggle to find any enthusiasm for a professional life after graduation. Then he explained how he had been given the chance to spend time with the people of Honduras. He remembered how he heard the girls' stories and how he worshipped with our sister church. He recalled how he wept, and how the Hondurans wept and prayed with him, over one girl who ran back into a life of prostitution. Then he added these words:

> There are many more stories of how God stretched my heart with those girls. I did not know how much I could love until God crammed close to thirty Honduran girls into my heart. It was almost overwhelming, I felt like I was yelling, "God! How many more?" to which He just smiled and said, "Until the whole world fits inside."

That is how you become rich toward God. Instead of cramming your barns, bedrooms, driveways, bank accounts, and attics full of stuff, let God cram your heart full of people to love in His name.

Chapter 10 Notes

CHAPTER ELEVEN

That's Me Prodding

We all fell to the ground, and I heard a voice saying to me in Aramaic, "Saul, Saul, why do you persecute me? It is hard for you to kick against the goads." — **Acts 26:14 (NIV)**

Come to me, all you who are weary and burdened, and I will give you rest. Take my yoke upon you and learn from me, for I am gentle and humble in heart, and you will find rest for your souls. For my yoke is easy and my burden is light. — **Matthew 11:28-30 (NIV)**

James Weldon Johnson compiled a book of poems based upon sermons that were traditionally preached in black churches. One line that was often uttered by black preachers was this: "Young man, young man, your arms are too short to box with the Lord."[14]

Christ was saying pretty much the same thing to Saul when He said, "It is hard for you to kick against the goads." This is not a popular verse. In all my years attending Sunday school and Vacation Bible School with its memory-verse competitions, I do not remember ever being asked to memorize this verse. I have seen dozens of samplers hung on the walls in Christian homes with verses like John 3:16 and Jeremiah 29:11, but I have never seen "It is hard for you to kick against the goads" on a wall. Nobody chooses this as his or her favorite verse.

This reference is actually Paul quoting Jesus. Paul had been arrested for preaching the gospel and was accused of causing a riot. He was thrown in jail and was now sharing his testimony and defense before King Agrippa. This verse is worth serious consideration for a couple of reasons.

First, the condition of our government or our world does not stop Jesus from speaking to us today. We may think the government we live under is corrupt, but it is nothing compared to what Paul had to deal with! The book of Acts says that Felix was pretty sure Paul was innocent of the charges for which he had been thrown in prison but still kept him there for two more years, "hoping that Paul would offer him a bribe" (Acts 24:26 NIV).

Second, Jesus is still talking! The encounter that Paul had with Jesus and the words Jesus spoke to him all took place several years after Christ had risen and ascended into heaven. Jesus has not stopped speaking into people's hearts and lives. And when He does speak, and we listen, it is always a life-changing experience.

How many of you remember where you were the day your children were born? All of you whom have been saved could tell me an awful lot about that day. In fact, you have probably shared the story over and over again and repeated word for word the things you heard Jesus say. That is no surprise.

Paul had a dramatic and life-altering conversation with Jesus, and he repeated the words often. In fact, this is the third time this story is told in the book of Acts. Jesus may have said many things to which we are not privy, but the Scriptures do record this interesting thing that Jesus said: "It is hard for you to kick against the goads."

A God Who Can Get Our Attention

Paul was not a believer when Jesus spoke to him. In fact, he couldn't have been further away from Jesus. His name then was Saul, and he hated Jesus, the gospel, and the church. He was fresh off of holding the coats for the men who stoned Stephen to death and hot on the trail of believers in Damascus whom he wanted to arrest and execute. So Saul wasn't exactly "sensitive" to the message of Jesus. He wasn't thinking about faith or exploring salvation. But God knows how to get our attention. When no preacher or worship leader could get Saul's attention, Jesus Himself came down and knocked Saul off his donkey and onto his (well, you know).

My Grandpa Chapin was a little bit like Saul. Not that he hated the church or Jesus. He didn't hate the church; he just wasn't interested in it. He didn't hate Jesus; he just didn't think much about Him at all. The whole business with Jesus, church, and faith seemed like a waste of time to my commonsense grandpa. However, when I began to preach at a little country church out in the middle of a cornfield in Indiana, he started to show up now and then. He would walk in, shake your hand, take a seat in the same pew, listen without much reaction, and exit pretty quickly after the "Amen." Then, one day, I received a phone call from my grandma telling me that grandpa had become a Christian. I wasn't sure I could believe it, so that evening, I drove over to his house.

We exchanged some small talk and then I worked up the nerve to ask Grandpa if it was true that he had been born again.

"Yes, Jack, it is. I finally decided that I needed to be saved," he said in his usual, direct way.

"Well, Grandpa, that is great. Can you tell me how and when it happened?" I asked.

I waited for him to share with me that it was the overwhelming conviction of one of my sermons that had finally broken down his resistance. Instead, he told me that one weekday he had been out working on their truck in his garage. He was leaning over the engine, stood up and cracked the crown of his head on the edge of the hood.

"Jack," he said shaking his head, "It hurt like crazy. I threw my tools on the floor, grabbed my head, and walked around cussing and swearing like a sailor for a few minutes."

The story continued. He collected himself and his tools and got back to work on his truck. After a few minutes, he raised up again and cracked his head on the exact same spot. Grandpa told me that he threw more tools and cussed a little louder this time. Once the pain subsided, he returned to his work. In a few more minutes, you guessed it—he stood up and cracked his head on the same spot for a third time.

"I was just about ready to go to cussing again, but then I stopped, and I bowed my head and I said, 'Okay Lord, I am listening.'"

I spent some time that day sharing the gospel together with my Grandpa, and we prayed with one another for the first time in my life. I left his house amazed at God and the ways that He uses to get people's attention.

And we desperately need Him to get our attention from time to time because we all have a tendency to wander aimlessly through this life He has given to us. Which is why I want you to consider two very odd, and seemingly unrelated, things that Jesus spoke of—a yoke and a goad.

We Were Designed to Serve God

Jesus spoke to Saul from heaven and said, "It is hard for you to kick against the goads" (Acts 26:14 NIV). Years before that, Jesus had issued this invitation to some who were listening to Him: "Take my yoke upon you." These were actually very common sayings in the culture. Everybody in the first century had used that phrase "kick against the goads" and had heard the phrase "take my yoke upon you." And when they used it, they knew that the word picture had to do with oxen.

A goad was a long stick, usually with some sort of point on the end, used by a farmer to poke oxen from the rear and get them moving, or from the side to change their direction. So when someone was feeling a "prodding" or an "urging" to take an action and they were resisting it, they were said to be "kicking against the goad." The yoke, of course, was the wood harness that would slip over the head and onto the shoulders of a team of oxen so that a farmer could direct them as they pulled a plow. You didn't use a goad or a yoke on a giraffe or a monkey because those are not domesticated animals. You use them on a domesticated animal that you have selected, purchased, and raised with a specific task for it to do.

God has a purpose for your life. God has selected you to serve some place in his field, and there are certain tools he uses to equip you to make that happen-a yoke and a goad. The yoke is about God's design for your life; the goad is about God's discipline in your life.

The First Tool—A Yoke

Take my yoke upon you and learn from me... — ***Matthew 11:29 (NIV)***

Yokes did not roll off of an assembly line. They were not mass-produced. They were handcrafted for a specific job and for the specific oxen that a farmer had to work with.

A few days after his dramatic encounter with Christ on the road to Damascus, Jesus sent a man named Ananias to see Paul and share this message: "The God of our ancestors has chosen you to know his will and to see the Righteous One and to hear words from his mouth. You will be a witness to all people of what you have seen and heard" (Acts 24:15-16). In the same way, the God who created us and purchased us with His blood has a designed plan for your life.

Some teachers have also pointed out that whenever a rabbi spoke of someone taking on their "yoke," it was an invitation for that person to learn from and follow him. To take on the yoke of Jesus then means that we do both—we learn His truth and we follow Him. Think about it. When a farmer puts the yoke on a team of oxen, what is the purpose? So that he can use that yoke to guide the oxen where he wants them to go and get them engaged in the work he needs them to do.

Jesus isn't in the business of fixing our problems and then turning us loose to return to doing whatever we want to do. Doing whatever we want is what messed us up so badly in the first place. It is why we were always laboring and burdened. We do not find the rest for our souls until we give up living how we want to live and submit to living how He directs us to live.

That is why it is critical for us to remember that serving Christ means having a relationship. Jesus says we learn from Him. We don't get stuff from Him and leave. We don't come to Him, place our religious orders, then dive impatiently back into our own agenda. When a farmer wanted to train a young, less experienced ox how to be effective as a work animal, he did it by yoking him in tandem with an older, more experienced one. The younger one learned by pulling together with the older one. When we enter a relationship with Jesus, we are committing to yoking up with Him. That means that for the rest of our lives we learn by paying attention to Him, feeling His moves, listening to His voice, and adjusting and responding to those things.

Not many of us want to operate that way. When I have discussions with other believers about the will of God for their lives, they most often take a Day-Timer approach rather than a relationship approach. They want God to reveal where He wants them to be five, ten, or twenty years from now. The problem with that is, if the Lord were to show you where He intends for you to be in ten years, then you would hear that, stop listening, and immediately begin trying to arrive at that destiny in your own way. God's will is as much about the trip as it is the destination. The Bible says, "The steps of a good man are ordered by the LORD" (Psalm 37:23 KJV). Steps—not calendars, planners, or day planners—are important in God's plan, and there are no shortcuts to His destinations for us.

Stop waiting for God to reveal His grand plan for you. Just get yoked up in relationship and start growing in your sensitivity to His leading. Respond to the day-by-day opportunities that appear. I cannot remember where I read it, but this line captures the truth perfectly: "I used to complain to the Lord how often my work was interrupted, until I realized that often the interruptions were His work." Living for the Lord means stopping and submitting your life to His control every day, getting yoked up with Him, and saying, "Today, Lord, guide me where You want me to go, make me responsive to when and where You want to turn, and help me to rely on Your strength with me, in me, beside me."

This approach will have great impact on our whole experience of life. Jesus says that if we submit to Him and yoke up with Him, we will find "rest for our souls." If we refuse, we will be "weary and heavy laden," or run down and worn out by life. At different times in my life, I have heard people speak about how hard it is to follow Christ and how difficult it can be to walk the narrow way. I understand. There is some accuracy in those observations. However, I have learned that no matter how hard it may be to be yoked up with Jesus, it is nowhere near as hard on us as when we insist on pulling through life on our own.

The Scriptures make it clear that we will have to learn how to endure many tests and trials along our way, but when you are pulling with Christ, there is a peace that stills you and fortifies you to keep moving. When Rosa Parks refused to give up her seat on a bus to a white person, she sparked a citywide bus boycott in the city of Selma. Dr. Martin Luther King told of how so many of the African American ladies who worked as maids in the city began walking to work instead of riding. During those walks, they would often be the target of heckling and abuse. He shared that one of those maids was being followed by a group of young men who keep snarling at her, "hey old lady, ain't your feet tired?" Finally, she turned to the group of boys and answered, "My feet are tired, but my soul is rested."

That captures the promise of a life lived harnessed to Jesus and submitted to His purpose. The yoke is His first tool.

The Second Tool—A Goad

> *It is hard for you to kick against the goads. — **Acts 26:14 (NIV)***

I noticed that Jesus said to Paul, "It is hard for you…" Christ was concerned about Paul. All of Paul's persecution and rebellion had not hurt Jesus. We do no harm to God if we choose to rebel against Him. We are making it hard on ourselves. All of us at times live like a big, dumb ox! We get willful. We resist the yoke of God. So, God has another tool, and that is the goad. He begins to poke and prod at our hearts to get us moving in the right direction.

> *When I kept silent, my bones wasted away through my groaning all the day long. For day and night your hand was heavy on me; my strength was sapped as in the heat of summer. Then I acknowledged my sin to you and did not cover up my iniquity. I said, "I will confess"…and you forgave the guilt of my sin. **(Psalms 32:3-5 NIV)***

If you try to play games with God and are resisting a direction you know you need to go, eventually God is going to lay His hands on you. And it will hurt. God has got some heavy hands. His hands will poke you awake at night, get in your pocket and snatch your prosperity, and stir you awake so you cannot sleep. They will snatch the joy right out of life for you.

His Motivation Is for Our Good

Remember Jesus's concern in Acts 26:14: In effect, He said, "this is hard for you, Saul. Why do you keep doing it?" Jesus always does what He does in our lives for our own good! The Bible tells us that the Lord disciplines people He loves. But do we trust Him enough to respond in His way?

We all tend to have a natural response to discipline. An ox will naturally kick back or resist in response to the prodding. So do we. As long as we keep resisting, God will keep prodding. So we have to ask ourselves: Will we learn anything? Will we respond? Or will we push back against God and say, "I am going to sleep with whomever I want" or, "I am going to hold onto this money, I earned it" or, "I will not go into ministry…I will not go have that conversation…I will not confess my sins and go to that altar"?

God sends the Holy Spirit to tell us things that are necessary—good changes that need to be made and actions we need to take. We respond by gritting our teeth and kicking that thought out of our heads or kicking that conviction out of our hearts. The only one who gets hurt in that is us. It is hard for us when we kick against the goads! It messes up our conscience and our peace.

I share all these things because I know that we all come to times when we feel the Lord poking us. We hear Him telling us to do things that sound absolutely crazy to us. He wants us to apologize when we feel we were the ones who were wronged. He wants us to end a habit, but we insist that someone explain rationally why we should. He is calling some of you to give up a career and enter ministry or mission, yet you keep trying to kick that thought into someday in the future.

I mean, look at Paul. What the Lord Jesus was asking him to believe and do was earth-shattering for him. It went against everything he had been taught to believe and was diametrically opposed to every doctrine to which he had devoted his life. In order to be obedient to God, Paul was going to have to throw his seminary degree, his ministry, and his friendships all out the window. He even tries to explain how difficult this was going to be to the Lord (read Acts 26:19-20).

However, he finally decided that no matter how crazy it sounded, it was the Lord speaking, so the only path for him was to listen and obey. The same is true for each of us. Jesus said, and still says, many things that cut against all our perceptions and plans, but the best response is not to argue or resist, but to admit that He is God and learn from Him how we should live.

Chapter 11 Notes

CONCLUSION

Faith Is Radical

Faith means that I try to listen to what my Lord says about every aspect of my life all the time—how I spend my money, how I raise my kids, how I treat my spouse, the quality of work I do for my employer, how I treat my customers, and the effort I put into teaching my students.

That transformative attitude is the goal of our faith. When Jesus comes to your soul, He wears His working clothes and He brings his tools with Him. Everything that God wants to do in your life, all the big words we throw around like *sanctification*, mean this: the goal of faith is simply to make you look like Jesus.

For God has a custom-designed plan for your life. He does not save us simply to rescue us from hell. God saves us to get us engaged in His purposes.

It may be a while before the choices you have made and the path God has asked you to follow produce any good in your life that is obvious to you or others. Yet make no mistake: Jesus can bring a radical change to any life, and that change is going to be thorough. The Lord is about total-life transformation

Through coming to know the real Jesus of Scripture, may we have the wisdom to see our selfishness, the humility to confess it and renounce it, and the courage to respond to God's new challenges in each new day.

REFERENCES

Notes

1. Lewis, C. S. "Charity" (ch. 9) in "Christian Behaviour" (book 3). *Mere Christianity*. 1952.
2. Buechner, Frederick. *A Room Called Remember: Uncollected Pieces*. New York: HarperCollins, 1992.
3. Tozer, A. W. "The Speaking Voice." *The Pursuit of God*. Harrisburg, PA: Christian Publications, 1948.
4. Swindoll, Charles R. "Strengthening Your Grip on Prayer." *Insight for Living Ministries: The Bible-Teaching Ministry of Charles R. Swindoll*. 18 March 2014. insight.org.
5. Willard, Dallas. *The Divine Conspiracy: Rediscovering Our Hidden Life in God*. San Francisco: HarperCollins, 1998.
6. Barclay, William. *The New Daily Study Bible*.
7. Peck, M. Scott. *The Road Less Traveled: A New Psychology of Love, Traditional Values and*

Spiritual Growth. New York: Simon & Schuster, 1978.

8. Lewis, C. S. "Forgiveness" (ch. 7) in "Christian Behaviour" (book 3). *Mere Christianity*. 1952.

9. Chesterton, G. K. *Orthodoxy*. 1908.

10. Scherker, Amanda. "...And 9 More Crazy Reasons People Divorced." *The Huffington Post*. 23 Jan. 2015. huffingtonpost.com.

11. Parrott, Les, and Leslie Parrott. *Love Talk: Speak Each Other's Language Like You Never Have Before*. Grand Rapids, MI: Zondervan, 2004.

12. Ortberg, John. *Dust of the Rabbi*.

13. MacDonald, Gordon. *Forging a Real World Faith*. Oliver-Nelson Books, 1989.

14. Johnson, James Weldon. *God's Trombones: Seven Negro Sermons in Verse*. New York: Viking, 1927.

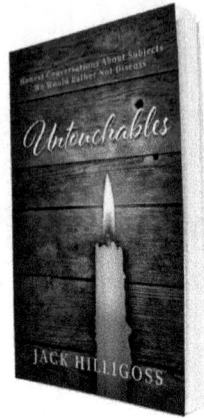

Equip yourself with practical and profound Christian responses to every "untouchable" topic! Get the book free at the link below.

https://jackhilligoss.com/get-untouchables

*1) **Click** the link*
*2) **Download and share** with others!*

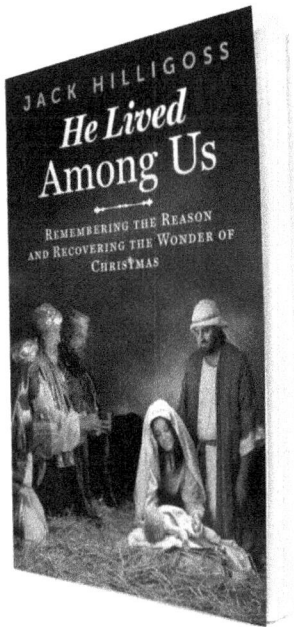

COMING CHRISTMAS 2016

Learn more at jackhilligoss.com

Christmas is a strange and powerful season.

Most of us have wrapped it up in lights and tinsel and buried it under stories of elves, flying reindeer, and a fat man in a red suit. Then we have left it in our closet of childhood memories to dust off each December as an escape from "real life."

But Christmas is not an escape or a fantasy. Christmas happened in "real life."

At Christmas, God lived among us—and He showed us how to live by living. It's time for us to follow His example!

About the Author

Jack Hilligoss is a husband, father, pastor, and Christ follower. He has been a pastor for 27 years, discipling and equipping believers from small churches in Midwestern cornfields to multicultural churches in the inner city, to a growing and community-impacting church in Lake Wales, Florida. During that time, he has learned that people are all very much the same. They have the same questions and they need the same hope. And, he has learned, everyone needs a pastor—someone who will help them think about life, someone who will show them how to hold their lives up to the light of Scripture and see from a perspective that may give them eternal meaning in the midst of the temporal rush of life. That is Jack's passion, and that is how he has spent his life.

About Sermon To Book

sermonto**book**
.com

SermonToBook.com began with a simple belief: that sermons should be touching lives, *not* collecting dust. That's why we turn sermons into high-quality books that are accessible to people all over the globe.

Turning your sermon series into a book exposes more people to God's Word, better equips you for counseling, accelerates future sermon prep, adds credibility to your ministry, and even helps make ends meet during tight times.

John 21:25 tells us that the world itself couldn't contain the books that would be written about the work of Jesus Christ. Our mission is to try anyway. Because, in Heaven, there will no longer be a need for sermons or books. Our time is now.

If God so leads you, we'd love to work with you on your sermon or sermon series.

Visit www.sermontobook.com to learn more.